5. Pauwls Church

5. yf Water house

S. Andre in Holborne

Paulus wharfe

Queene hythe

The 3 Cranes

the Eel Ships

T H

Winchester house

SHAKESPEARE'S FLOWERING OF THE SPIRIT

MARGARET BENNELL

END PAPERS:
Front – Part of the Long View of London from Bankside, Wenceslaus Hollar, 1647
Rear – The Globe Theatre; The Swan Theatre after a sketch by de Witt 1596

FRONTISPIECE:
William Shakespeare by William Blake

Acknowledgments are due to the Manchester City Art Galleries for the Frontispiece, to the British Museum and Messrs Batsford Ltd for the end papers and to the following publishers and authors for permission to quote from various books:

Collins, from "Dr Zhivago" by Boris Pasternak.
Faber and Faber Ltd, from Stephen Spender's Collected Poems.
A. C. Harewood, from "Shakespeare's Prophetic Mind".
Rudolf Steiner Nachlassverwaltung, from Rudolf Steiner's writings.

LAYOUT:
Arne Klingborg

The Lanthorn Press acknowledges most gratefully the grant given by the Cotswold Chine School for this production of *Shakespeare's Flowering of the Spirit*.

Printed by Affordable Print Ltd, Cornwall
ISBN 0-906155-02-9

SHAKESPEARE'S FLOWERING OF THE SPIRIT

by
MARGARET BENNELL

Edited and Completed
by
ISABEL WYATT

WILLIAM SHAKESPEARE BY WILLIAM BLAKE

I think continually of those who were truly great,
Who, from the womb, remembered the soul's history
Through corridors of light where the hours are suns,
Endless and singing. Whose lovely ambition
Was that their lips, still touched with fire,
Should tell of the spirit, clothed from head to foot in song.
     What is precious is never to forget …
Never to allow gradually the traffic to smother
With noise and fog the flowering of the spirit.

STEPHEN SPENDER

CONTENTS

CONTENTS

FOREWORD

The contents of this book have arisen out of three lecture-courses given at Hawkwood College, Stroud, in recent years – *The Christian Mysteries of Europe*, in which I collaborated with Willi Sucher and Hans van der Stok, and *The Chymical Wedding of Christian Rosenkreutz* and *William Shakespeare*, in both of which I collaborated with Isabel Wyatt. The aspects explored in this last course (undertaken in connection with the Quartercentenary in 1964) aroused a deep urge in us both to carry further our researches into the spiritual content and esoteric background of Shakespeare's plays.

To all three collaborators I would like to offer my warm thanks.

Above all, deep gratitude is due to Rudolf Steiner, whose world-outlook and whose studies in history and literature have formed a foundation for this work.

This book is to be regarded as only a tentative beginning, a stimulus to others to work further along these lines, so that Shakespeare's plays may become what we believe they were meant by destiny to be become – a source of guidance and inspiration to modern mankind.

JULY, 1966   MARGARET BENNELL

EDITORIAL NOTE

Margaret Bennell died before the completion of this book, and I have completed and revised the text in accordance with her instructions.

ISABEL WYATT

PART ONE

THE SOUL'S HISTORY:
THE MAN

CHAPTER I

SHAKESPEARE'S DESCENT FROM THE MYSTERIES

"That which is generally known as the Drama, that which is felt by the Western world to be dramatic art, and which reached its culminating point in Shakespeare, is a stream of spiritual life having its source in the Ancient Mysteries; it is a secularisation of the Ancient Mysteries. If we trace dramatic art back to its cradle, we find it in the Ancient Mysteries, such as those of Eleusis".

RUDOLF STEINER[1]

EUROPEAN DRAMA took its rise in the Mysteries of Eleusis. There candidates for initiation were taught in living picture-form how the gods intervene in the life of men on earth, and what mankind would have to experience inwardly in future epochs.
In these Mysteries, and in attending the plays of the three great tragedians who later stemmed from them, men underwent a catharsis, as a result of their heightened experiencing of compassion and awe.[2]
The Mystery Drama of Eleusis conveyed to the mystae (those seeking initiation) the secrets of life, death and resurrection. Persephone, the pure, unfallen human soul, was carried off by Hades into the realm of darkness, suffering and death. In the night that intervened between one act of the drama and the next, the mystae experienced the terrors of what in Christian terminology might be

[1] WONDERS OF THE WORLD
[2] Aristotle: POETICS VI

called Purgatory. (This is referred to in more detail in Chapter XIII.)

After searching in agonised distress for her lost daughter, Demeter conceived a new god. The mystae saw the Mother in a blaze of light, holding in her arms the Child, Jacchos-Dionysos. (The name Jacchos means *Born of Light*.) Answering Persephone's cry of distress which rose to him from the depths, he became her saviour, restoring her to her rightful place in heaven.

In the Greek world this wonderful Mystery Drama prefigured the birth of Christ at about the same time as, among the Jews, the Hebrew prophets were foretelling the coming of the Messiah.

Æschylos (525-456 B.C.) was the first dramatist to bring a full Mystery-Drama out from the Eleusinian Mysteries on to an open stage. For this deed he was summoned before the chief judges of Athens, and narrowly escaped the fate of Socrates for having, as they said, betrayed the Mysteries.

His tragedies all show the working of destiny. In his *Prometheus Bound* he portrays the blessing and the curse of egohood, and shows how, at its birth, it feels cut off from its fellows and from communion with the gods. (We see how, in the picture, the intensified experience of modern man is already foreshadowed here.)

As a result, the ego (Prometheus) becomes a fettered prisoner until redeemed by "one who dies voluntarily." Herakles, the deliverer, is thus also in this connection a prefiguring of Christ.

The second of the three great tragedians was Sophocles (495-406 B.C.), the finest of whose works (as we know them today) was the *Œdipus* trilogy. He showed the dolorous situation of the ego as it loses the support of the blood-tie and has not yet learnt to stand alone. After years of blindness and misery, Œdipus dies a tragic death.

But the third part of the trilogy shows the triumph of the selfless ego. Antigone, the Eternal-Feminine, is unconquerable through her power of sacrificial love.

Euripides (480-405 B.C.) was the youngest of this great trio of dramatists. His was a logical consciousness, already becoming more at home in concepts than in pictures.

It was in his plays that the word "conscience"was heard for the first time. Only a few years earlier, Aeschylus had shown Orestes, after murdering his father, pursued by avenging spiritual beings – the Erinys, the Furies. Euripides, portraying the same story, shows Orestes tormented by an inner voice.

The friend of Orestes asks:

"What aileth thee? What sickness ruineth thee?"

Orestes replies:

"Conscience! To know that I have wrought a fearful deed."

It indicates a momentous change in consciousness when a man who has done wrong no longer feels forces outside himself as his accusers, but has awakened within his own soul a new faculty which condemns him.

It was known in the Rosicrucian teachings of Shakespeare's day that the three qualities – conscience, awe and compassion – called forth in this way by Greek Drama would be those by which man today and in the future would influence most strongly the evolution of the Earth. We shall see later how these qualities are reflected in the pilgrim's progress of Shakespeare's plays.

After Euripides, Greek Drama became satirical, and presently declined. Roman Drama had never attempted to portray spiritual events, and after a period of brilliance fell into decadence. For some centuries, Drama ceased to exist in Europe as a stream of spiritual life.

When it began to be revived, it was in the very simplest and most naïve of forms, and within the bosom of the Christian Church. It seems singularly fitting that the first seeds of the resurrection of Drama should come forth from the Resurrection Tomb. For in the tenth century, two priests attired as angels were shown sitting by the Easter Sepulchre on Easter morning; three other priests attired as the Three Marys approached the angels, who said to them:

"Whom do you seek in the sepulchre, O Christian women?"

The Three Marys replied:

"Jesus of Nazareth, Who was crucified, O heavenly ones."

Then the angels told them the glad tidings:

"He is not here. He has risen, even as He foretold. Go; announce that He is risen from the sepulchre."

In these tableaux were the small beginnings of a new religious Drama.

The plays which grew out of these tableaux came to be known as Mystery Plays. The name is said in this case to be derived from *mystère*, and this in turn from *ministère*, clergy, because it was the priests who made them and originally played in them. Yet they also have a certain claim to be Mystery Plays in the Eleusinian sense, since, in their homely fashion, they dramatise the great scope of Man's evolution as recounted in the Old and New Testaments, setting the Crucifixion on Golgotha at its central turning point, and, from this, looking backward to the Creation, and forward to the Last Judgement.

As "in Æschylos and in Sophocles we already see the artistic elements, as it were, lifted out from the Mysteries,"[3] so, on its humbler level, this young Western European

[3] Rudolf Steiner: SHAKESPEARE AND THE NEW IDEALS
(Lecture given at Stratford-on-Avon in April, 1922)

Drama now followed the same path. Its Mystery Plays dramatised the Scripture narrative; they moved in the sphere of the supersensible. The Mystery Plays which grew out of them dramatised incidents in the lives of the saints and martyrs; heaven was still present, but the human being had moved to the centre of the stage. In the Morality Plays which followed in turn, the characters were no longer human beings but personified Virtues and Vices.

In both Mystery Play and Miracle Play there had been light relief; into the awe-inspiring, comedy was interwoven. In the play *Noah's Flood*, for example, Noah's wife has a shrewish tongue; in the play of the *Nativity*, the Shepherds provide rustic fun; there are "devils and devices in plenty to delight the eye and ear."

But now these two elements part company; solemnity goes the way of the Morality Play, and the comic impulse is directed into yet another new dramatic form – the Interlude. And with the Interlude, secular drama makes its appearance.

The secularization is not confined to the subject-matter of the plays. As we have seen, in this rebirth of Drama the priests (as at Eleusis) had been the first actors; it was born literally within the four walls of the Church.

From the fourteenth century onwards, it takes the first step away from her into the outside world. The Mystery Plays are still played under the aegis of the Church, but they are acted now by members of the Craftsmen's Guilds. To each Guild is assigned its own highly appropriate play – to the Goldsmith's, the *Three Kings*; to the Shipwrights, *Noah's Flood*; to the Bakers, the *Last Supper*; to the Vintners, the *Marriage at Cana*; to the Bedmakers, the *Dream of Pilate's Wife*; to the Fishmongers, *Jonah and the Whale*; to the Cooks (famed for their

Hell-Mouth noises, beaten on cooking-pots), the *Harrowing of Hell*.

The players, if secular, are still amateur, and still under the direction of the church. But with the Interlude a new portent appears – the professional actor. With him that trickle which was to grow into the main stream of Western European Drama flowed away from the Church and out into the world to seek its fortune.

The religious plays had been played first inside the Church; then in the churchyard; then in the market-place; then in "appointed places all about the town." The new secular drama, faring out into the world, had to fashion for itself a new secular stage, find itself new playing-places.

The religious plays went the round of the appointed places all about the town on pageants, great six-wheeled wagons drawn by four or six horses. At each appointed place two such pageants were rolled together end to end, giving a roomy acting-space. To this actors came up from the tiring room below the stage by two trap-doors in the floor, over each of which was an openwork house. The one to Stage Right, two storeys high, represented Heaven; the one to Stage Left, Hell's Mouth; the space between was Middle Earth. Thus this Mystery Play stage was a microcosm for the ecclesiastical macrocosm.

Because Heaven's Tower was to the right, everything which stood for the element of good was stationed on that side; because Hell's Mouth was to the left, this was the side of Evil. Thus, in the plays of the *Three Kings*, the stable at Bethlehem stood beneath Heaven's Tower, Herod's Palace stood at Hell's Mouth, and the Three Kings met in the space between; while in the play of *Daniel*, Daniel's house was in Heaven's Tower, Belshazzar's throne was over Hell's Mouth, in between stood the lion's den, and all was in view throughout the play.

All also was in view from all four sides of the pageant. There was no front-stage, back-stage, backdrop, curtain. The play was in the round; and, "being all open at the sides and top, all beholders might see and hear it."

Such pageant-wagons the professional players now took with them on their travels. They would set them up in the middle of an inn-yard, where the "penny ground-lings" could stand all round the stage, but where, also, if you were willing to pay twopence, you could watch the play from a seat in the galleries of rooms running one above the other round the enclosed courtyard. The Boar's Head, the Cross-Keys, the Bell, the Black Bull, the Red Bull were among the London inns which became famous as such improvised theatres.

London also had its bear-pits, where, on non-bear-baiting days, the pageant-stage could be set up, to be "circled about with wonder of all eyes." Here, indeed, it literally was a circle, for the bear-pits were round; and it was discovered that this circular shape vastly improved the acoustics.

So when, in 1576 (Shakespeare being then twelve years old), James Burbage built England's first playhouse for those "tragedies of blood" which were splendid and sensational first fruits of Elizabethan Drama, he built it round, like the bear-pits, with tiers of galleries, like the innyards; and its stage was modelled on the Mystery pageant-stage, with open framework houses to right and left, still called Heaven's Tower and Hell's Mouth, stage and galleries roofed, and the pit, still with standing room only, still open to the sky. (Today we still speak of *pit* and *gallery* and – despite our modern theatre's angularity – upper *circle*).

This, then, was the theatre as Shakespeare found it

awaiting him nine years later, when he arrived on James Burbage's doorstep with a horse to sell and his genius to place at evolution's service.The downward recapitulation was complete; Drama had again descended from the supersensible and come out on to the open stage of Earth. Now, Man having reached a later stage of consciousness, Drama was ready to be led along a path of completely new unfolding. And Shakespeare had come to London to unfold it.

CHAPTER II

SHAKESPEARE'S ENGLAND

"In Shakespeare there is at work more than a single human personality – there is at work the spirit of his century, and with it the spirit of the whole of human evolution".

RUDOLF STEINER[4]

W E know that the destiny of any great man brings him to earth at an appointed place at an appointed time; and we have seen how Shakespeare came to earth just when the new drama-form in which he was to work out the task he had come to do had been forged and lay ready to his hand.

Now we may ask further: What part had sixteenth century England in what Laurens van der Post calls this "togetherness in time"? Into what kind of England did he come? What were its people's hopes and fears? What world-picture was theirs? To what elements in their soul-history was his own soul-history relevant?

England had not long emerged from civil war – from those Wars of the Roses in which the old nobility had been all but wiped out. A great body of medieval tradi-

[4] SHAKESPEARE AND THE NEW IDEALS

tion had died with them. The new nobility created by the King had included many successful merchants, who brought a practical bourgeois commonsense to their new station, thus preparing the ground, long ahead, for a later utilitarian – and, indeed, industrial – era.

After Henry VIII's quarrel with Rome, religion had become a burning question. The reigns of Edward VI and Mary had left the country suspended between the two extremes of Catholic and Puritan. England lay under the fear of Catholic Spain.

What would be her fate at the hands of the young Princess Elizabeth? Beyond imposing fines for non-attendance at church, the new queen wisely did nothing. A great stride had been taken in the direction of religious freedom, itself a step towards that isolation out of which alone the ego can be fully born.

When, in 1588, the Spanish Armada was overcome, as if by a miracle, dispelling the monstrous nightmare which had for so long hung over the nation, this was swept by a wave of near-worship for the Queen, and for a few years England became Merrie England, filled with rose-colour, dancing, song.

This intoxication was heightened by new vistas in space opened by exploration and discovery. Drake navigated the world and brought back Spanish treasure. Raleigh dreamed of an Empire for his Virgin Queen. Travellers brought back fabulous plants, animals, men, and even more fabulous travellers' tales. The world was suddenly revealed as greater, richer, stranger than men's wildest imaginings had conceived.

The Renaissance had unveiled equally far-reaching vistas in time. The unguessed riches of Greece and Rome were as suddenly opened up. All this was like heady wine as it met, and at fist mingled with, the cherished beliefs of the medieval world-picture.

But presently these were to be shattered by its workings. Erasmus spoke as a true prophet when he said that the introduction of the teaching of the classics into schools was like bringing the wooden horse into Troy.

One of the most firmly established of these convictions had been that of a World Order, a Chain of Being stretching without a break from God's throne to the meanest creature, with fire similarly the highest among the elements, the sun among the planets, the eagle among birds, the lion among beasts, the king among men. How fundamental this cosmic order was is described by Ulysses in *Troilus and Cressida*:

The heavens themselves, the planets and this centre
Observe degree, priority and place,
Insisture, course, proportion, season, form,
Office, and custom, in all line of order.
And therefore is the glorious planet Sol
In noble eminence enthron'd and spher'd
Amidst the other; whose med'cinable eye
Corrects the ill aspects of planets evil,
And posts, like the commandment of a king,
Sans check, to good and bad –
*   – O, when degree is shak'd,*
Which is the ladder to all high designs,
The enterprise is sick. How could communities,
Degrees in schools, and brotherhoods in cities,
The Primogenitive and due of birth,
Prerogative of age, crowns, sceptres, laurels,
But by degree, stand in authentic place?
Take but degree away, untune that string,
And, hark! What discord follows.

(I,iii)

Such a world-picture made for optimism; men felt themselves held secure in an ordered universe of which the
earth was the centre, a universe to which man owned his
origin and his destiny, and to whom man was its sole
charge and care.

But now there happened two shattering events.

One was the announcement of Copernicus that this was
not so; that it was the sun which held this proud central
position, so that the earth dwindled into an insignificant
body cast out into a corner of an uncaring cosmos.

The other was the translation of Machiavelli's *Il Principe*,
which had already, when published in Italy in 1532,
spread pessimism like a blight there.

"Whoever desires," he wrote, "to govern a state must
start by assuming that all men are bad and ever ready
to show their vicious nature." A strong ruler who was bad
was better that a weak ruler who was good. Compassion
and love in the heart of a ruler could be drawbacks. Each
man must stand alone, think only of himself.

The impact of this doctrine was wide-spread and cata-
clysmic. Machiavelli was quoted some four hundred
times by Elizabethan writers, often with hysterical re-
pudiation. But the seeds of doubt were sown. Might it
not, after all, be true that a personal virtue could be a
social fault?

We can see Shakespeare wrestling with this problem in
his historical plays. Henry VI is a saint, but a worthless
king; Richard III is the type of a new man, aptly called
by John Danby a machiavel.

Richards says:

> *But since the heavens have shaped my body so,*
> *Let Hell make crooked my mind to answer it.*

I have no brother, I am like no brother,
And this word (Love), which greybeards call divine,
Be resident in men like another,
But not in me. I am my self alone.

(Richard III, V, vi)

Yet towards the close of the play he feels the desolation of utter loneliness:

I shall despair. There is no creature loves me,
And if I die, no soul shall pity me.

*(*V, iii)

Shakespeare already shows in Hamlet the dichotomy of the new outlook brought about by the impact of Copernican astronomy and the Machiavellian doctrine:

I have of late, but wherefore I know not, lost
all my mirth ... and indeed, it goes so heavily
with me that this goodly frame, the earth, seems
to me a sterile promontory; this most excellent
canopy, the air, look you, this brave, overhanging
firmament, this majestical roof fretted with
golden fire, why, it appears no other thing
to me than a foul and pestilential canopy of vapours.
What a piece of work man is! How noble in
reason! How infinite in faculty! in form,
in moving, how express and admirable! in
action how like an angel in apprehension
how like a god! The beauty of the world, the
paragon of animals; and yet, to me, what is
this quintessence of dust?

(Hamlet, II, ii)

This dichotomy had already been lamented by Sir John
Davis in 1599:

"I know myself a man,
Which is a proud and yet a wretched thing."

Donne, a little later, was to record the undermining of
a whole world-conception:

"The new philosophy calls all in doubt ...
' Tis all in pieces, all coherence gone."

And Calvin was to cry out against the consequent futility
of life:

"A shapeless ruin is all that remains."

In truth, what was happening was no less than a change
of consciousness. An older mankind had felt itself held
secure by a cosmos that cared for it; the new man felt
cut off from the heavens, standing in complete loneliness
of soul.
A man who felt himself but a quintessence of dust had
little cause to value or to practise virtue. Such a man,
after several attempts, Shakespeare portrayed to perfec-
tion in Edmund in *King Lear*, – cold, calculating contemp-
tuous, unscrupulous in his pursuit of his own selfish ends.

This sudden awareness of schism within himself shocked the man of the age into new self-discovery. He began to seek for self-knowledge of the emerging individuality. We know how, for example, Rembrandt and Dürer painted self-portraits, each gazing intently at his own countenance as if asking the searching questions: "Who am I? What am I?" In Valentine, Romeo, Jaques, Hamlet, Posthumous and Prospero, one feels that Shakespeare has also painted portraits of at least aspects of himself in his youth, young middle age and maturity.

The soul which asked of itself: "Who am I?" asked also of its fellows: "Who are you?" It has been said of the portraits of Shakespeare and his contemporaries that they are portraits of souls experiencing the shock of meeting ego to ego.

It is significant that historical plays bulk so largely in Shakespeare's earlier work; for it is precisely when self-awareness is being stirred that history takes on meaning and perspective. That self-awareness was being stirred on a large scale is evident from the fact that Hall and Holinshed, Shakespeare's two great source-books for his Histories, were read voraciously; they were the staple diet of merchants, and are mentioned among the furnitures of palaces, where they were left about in waiting-rooms, as dentists now leave *Punch*.

Much in the plays themselves that is not clear to us was perfectly so to Elizabethan audiences, for to them these were stage-versions of their favourite reading – good doses of Hall and Holinshed, magnificently dramatised. Yet they were infinitely more than fine chronicle-plays; there are signs that Shakespeare was already penetrating to the invisible forces working behind visible events, for out of his inspired handling of his massive material emerged a picture of the weaving of destiny in English

history, on the one hand as an epitome of world-history,
and on the other as a prologue to contemporary changes
in consciousness.

And now, in accordance with these changes, Shakespeare
re-shapes Drama into an objective study of the single
personality.

"Shakespeare's dramas are above all character-dramas.
The great interest they arouse does not lie so much in the
action as in the wonderful exposition and development
of the single characters. The poet conjures up before us a
human character and unfolds its thoughts and feelings.
"These character-dramas could only arise as a result of
the higher estimation of the individual during the Renaissance. The Christian type of the Middle Ages (Dante for
example) was not concerned with the single personality.
A new-world conception aroused interest in the individual
human being. Shakespeare's quick fame shows that the
audience had an interest in the representation of personality. He presents individual, not ethical or moral
ideas …

His plays act through the power which lies in the description of the single character. It is this which constitutes
their living essence, which has never been surpassed
throughout the centuries."[5]

We see, then, that Shakespeare was born at a crucial
moment in the life of England, when Elizabethan man
was just crossing the dread boundary between medieval
age and modern. It was Shakespeare's task to mediate
this crossing.

Here, then, is at work in him "the spirit of his century".
But where can we see the working of "the spirit of the
whole of human evolution"?

Shakespeare guards that point in the evolution of consciousness when the incarnation of the individual ego,

---

[5] Rudolf Steiner: SHAKESPEARE. (Lecture given in Berlin in 1902)

foretold in the Ancient Mysteries, foreshadowed in the first Greek dramatists, has to be achieved in a new and far-reaching way. It is all too easy for the new man, cut off from the brooding care of the cosmos, to become an Edmund. But the new man was meant to become a being of integrity, capable of unselfish love and of making free decisions, clear-sighted and objective as regards his fellows. So alongside Edmund he portrays Cordelia.

He shows us how differently this self-awareness of the ego is expressed by differing sorts and conditions of men, at different stages of soul-development.

There is Richard III's loveless

> *I am my self alone.*
>
> *(Richard III, V, vi)*

Or again, his

> *Richard loves Richard, that is, I am I.*
>
> *(Richard III, V, iii)*

There is the Bastard Falconbridge's consciousness of the uniqueness of the individual:

> *And I am I, howe'er I was begot.*
>
> *(King John, I, i)*

There are Hamlet's painful probings of the problems of the ego:

> *What is a man? ... How stand I then,*
> *That have a father kill'd, a mother stained, ...*
> *And let all sleep?*
>
> *(Hamlet, IV, iv)*

There is Regan's callous but penetrating comment on her
father:

> *He hath ever but slenderly known himself*
> *(King Lear*, I, i)

And there is that father's piteous

> *Who is it who can tell me who I am?*
> *(King Lear*, I, iv)

And, because tragedy can bring self-knowledge, there is
Lear's achievement of self-knowledge in the end:

> *I am a very foolish fond old man;*
> *And, to deal plainly,*
> *I fear I am not in my perfect mind.*
> *(King Lear*, IV, vii)

There is the Duke of Vienna, on a path of spiritual
striving, whom Escalus describes as

> *On that, above all other strifes, contended*
> *especially to know himself.*
> *(Measure for Measure*, III, ii)

There is Oliver, aware of such a path:

> CELIA: *Was't you who did so oft contrive to kill him?*

OLIVER: *'Twas I, but 'tis not I. I do not shame*
To tell you what I was, since my conversion
So sweetly tastes, being the thing I am.

(As You Like It, IV, iii)

There is "holy Gonzalo",watching growth in self-knowledge:

Ferdinand found a wife
Where he himself was lost
... And Prospero a kingdom
In a poor isle, and all of us ourselves
When no man was his own

(The Tempest, V, i)

There is Florizel, steadfast under paternal pressure:

I am but sorry, not afear'd, delay'd
But nothing altered. What I was, I am.

(The Winter's Tale, IV, iv)

And Florizel again, having pierced the ego's inmost secret:

I cannot be
Mine own, nor anything to any, if
I be not thine.

(The Winter's Tale, IV, iv)

We who are not of his century are still of Shakespeare's age. With us the ego is still in a state of becoming. He reveals in his plays the manifold steps of this becoming in their due order within the large sweep of the soul's history of mankind, placing before us pictures of the long strides from stepping-stone to stepping-stone which brought us to where we are now. He shows us, for example, how the world of Lear had to pass away before that of Hamlet could be born, and how in the world which struggles to be born with Hamlet's struggles, Ferdinand's and Miranda's love was a sealing of their fathers' own new finding of each other's true beings in friendship, while in the world ruled by the Lear-consciousness, before their love could bring their fathers together Romeo and Juliet had had to die.

Those stages on the ego's becoming which were proclaimed prophetically in the Eleusinian Mysteries and in the early Greek dramas which proceeded from them, Shakespeare recapitulates from a later vantage-point. But in the journey from B.C. to A.D. they have traversed Golgotha, and in being Christened they have been transmuted.

We can understand, then, why Goethe speaks of Shakespeare as an interpreter of the World-Spirit; we can feel that in him there is indeed working the spirit of the whole of evolution.

CHAPTER III

THE MERMAID TAVERN

"The continuous currents that flow through human evolution from the Ancient Mysteries and their cults Shakespeare took entirely into his inner life, and his plays come forth like dreams which are awake and real".

RUDOLF STEINER[6]

E have seen how the stream of Drama which took its rise in the Ancient Mysteries had lost its spiritual content by the time of Roman playwrights such as Seneca and Plautus. But other streams arising from the same sources preserved their spiritual content longer – long enough to unite with the Christianity whose coming they had formerly proclaimed, and in that union to be transmuted. In this way a stream of ancient wisdom proceeding from the Mysteries of Ephesus reappeared in Christian times, transmuted into the Grail-Stream. This stream changes from century to century according to human needs. Thus, it found a first continuation in Templar Wisdom, which in turn flowed, along with other streams from past ages, into Rosicrucianism, so that one could say that into this was absorbed the whole Christianised religious wisdom of that time.

[6] SHAKESPEARE AND THE NEW IDEALS

Christian Rosenkreutz, who brought it into being, was born on 1378. In 1406, when he was twenty-eight years old, he left Middle Europe on a seven-year pilgrimage over all the known world, visiting both its pre-Christian Mystery Temples and its Christian holy places,culminating at Damascus in a Christian initiation which repeated the Damascus Experience of St. Paul.

In 1413 he returned to Europe, having absorbed in these centres the essence of their teachings, which, by the afterworkings of powerful inner contemplation, was transformed and brought forth in a new form as an esoteric current of Christianity – that synthesis of all religions, philosophies and schools of wisdom which became the content of the Rosicrucian movement as he inaugurated it in 1459. He died in 1484 at the age of a hundred and six.

We have seen how the Renaissance heralded a new epoch in European evolution. In this personality we can see a channel used by the spiritual powers of the age directing and guarding these changes. In his quest for the Spirit behind Nature and for the Spirit in Man we can see new connections being forged between the heavenly world and men whom the new self-awareness, the dawning sciences and increasing materialism were to drive deeper into the earthly one.

For this reason we find his teachings being extensively studied in the sixteenth and seventeenth centuries, not only by men of personal piety, of the stuff of saints and mystics, but also by many of the most enlightened and responsible thinkers of the time.

In England the Elizabethan age was one of the most brilliant periods in our literature. A galaxy of exceptional minds were met together, many of whom could find a spiritual home neither in the newly challenged Catholic

faith nor among Puritans with souls scoured bare as
their conventicales.

These exceptional minds were full of questions and
questings. What more natural then, than that they
should turn, some perhaps with little more than intellectual curiosity, but more with seriously seeking souls, to
this vast mind-enlarging and life-creating body of esoteric
teaching?

The centre of intellectual London was the Mermaid
Tavern. There nearly all the intelligentsia were to be
met – Raleigh, Sidney, Spenser, Lyly, Marlowe, Kyd,
Penry, Greene, Nashe, Chester, Beaumont, Chapman,
Heywood, Marston, Ben Jonson and a host of others –
scholars, poets and playwrights, and courtiers when the
Queen was in residence. There one can picture them
sitting and discussing, in their nimble and fiery fashion,
Plato's World of Ideas, or Alchemy, or the meaning of
Greek myths, or the Gay Science, or the Nature of Man,
or the Temple Legend, or Rosicrucian Initiation, or
Cathar Manicheism, or Divine Intelligences, or Hermetic
philosophy, or the Diana Mysteries of Ephesus, or the
Phoenix Mysteries of Tyre, "till the birds sang in the
morning."

For the Elizabethans were intensively *alive* in their thinking. As we saw with their reaction to Machiavelli's *The
Prince*, to them a thought was not an abstraction; it was
an experience.

Into this climate came that child of Nature, Shakespeare,
straight from England's rural heart. When, after his
meteoric rise from horse-boy to playwright, he found a
place within the Mermaid's circle, he found his spiritual
home. These metamorphosed "continual currents from
the Ancient Mysteries" he was able to take so "entirely

into his inner life" because, in the Platonic sense, they were already there. He absorbed them with (In Yeats' phrase) "an understanding born from a deeper fountain than thought."

In 1459, when Christian Rosenkreutz was a little over eighty years of age, that experience came to him which resulted in his founding of his Order. The account of it which has come down to us, called *The Chymical Wedding of Christian Rosenkreutz* and couched in Mystery pictures, was written down in 1604 by Valentin Andreae, a seventeen-year-old student at Tübingen University (later to become a Lutheran pastor), and first published in Strasbourg in 1616. But an oral version would seem to have had wide circulation for some years before that, for the story would seem to have been already known in London in 1589.[7]

Shakespeare had come to London in 1585, at the age of twenty-one, when the ego comes to birth. Has not this concurrency the hallmark of yet another "togetherness in time"?

As its title suggests, *The Chymical Wedding* (like *Flor and Blanchefleur* and the Seventh Book of Malory's *Morte d'Arthur*, recounting the adventures of Sir Gareth), is told in terms of alchemy, a pursuit which had had a lengthy and chequered history in England. In the reign of Edward III, the possibility of turning base metals into gold had been seriously enquired into by the Officials of the Mint, only, in 1403, to be declared a felony. Nevertheless, Henry VI had appointed a Commission to review the matter, hoping that "the craft of multiplying gold and silver"might be induced to replenish his depleted treasury.

In the reign of Elizabeth, alchemists were common, and

[7] Paul Arnold, ESOTÉRISME DE SHAKESPEARE

cheats and frauds more so. They are satirised in Ben Jonson's play, *The Alchemist*; at the same time the cheat in it gives a serious explanation of what the alchemist is really seeking. In *The Chymical Wedding*, too, Christian Rosenkreutz is pained to find cheats at the wedding-feast: "As they grew warm with wine, these guests of the lewder sort began to vaunt of their abilities; one heard the movements of the Heavens, the second could see Plato's Ideas, the third could number the atoms of Democritus. One could prove this, another that; and commonly the most sorry idiots made the loudest noise."

For what the genuine Rosicrucian alchemist was seeking was something on quite another level – it was nothing less than the birth of the higher self in the soul, and the purifying of the up-building formative forces in man and the healing of the fallen nature of his body until, in the far future, the Philosopher's Stone could be achieved. In *The Chymical Wedding*, Christian Rosenkreutz relates how he is permitted, in the Tower of Olympus, to help in the fashioning of these clear bodies of the future for the young King and Queen:

"When we opened our two little moulds, we found two bright and almost transparent little images, angelically fair babes, a male and a female, each being but four inches long, and beheld them till we were almost besotted upon so exquisite an object. When they had reached their perfect full growth, with curled yellow hair, our Virgin entered with two curious garments, which could have been crystal but that they were gentle and not transparent ..." meanwhile, below, the rejected alchemists were "industriously blowing at furnaces and making gold, imagining they were herein wonderfully preferred before us."

Such natural substances as salt, mercury and sulphur,

and their metamorphoses in the alchemist's laboratory, were for the genuine alchemist outward symbols of aspects of the path of inner development he strove to follow. Thus, since in Nature salt preserves from decay, and in man the desires and passions were seen as forces leading to decay, "the process of conquering these forces through pure thoughts directed to the spiritual was seen as a microcosmic salt-forming process. So this Nature-process became for the medieval Rosicrucian a form of devout prayer."[8]

Alchemical pictures, then, were the veil true alchemists hung before the eyes of the vulgar to shield the delicate processes of initiation from their ignorant understanding. It is of such initiation that *The Chymical Wedding* tells.

Robert Fludd (1574-1637), perhaps the best-known and best-respected of Elizabethan Rosicrucians, wrote that Rosicrucian wisdom released men's minds from the narrow bonds of Catholics and Puritans without their ceasing to be true Protestants. But the strait-laced Puritans who in Shakespeares' day held the power in the City Council regarded the frequenters of the Mermaid as rank heretics and the Mermaid herself as a little hotbed of atheism.The fact that what was discussed there with such avidity was part of the climate of intellectual Europe, engrossing some of its best and most enlightened minds as well as its purest hearts, merely added fuel to their fire.

In 1593 they decided to send a Puritan preacher to con-vert the Mermaid circle, who, with more exuberance than tact, returned him with a gag of tar and wax. The enraged City Fathers felt the time had come for stronger measures. They imprisoned two of the less circumspect and more choleric members, Kyd and Marlowe. Kyd was strangled in prison.

[8] Rudolf Steiner, ROSICRUCIAN CHRISTIANITY

After a trial before the Star Chamber, in which he brilliantly defended himself against the charge of atheism, Marlowe was set free. A few days later he was stabbed in a tavern in Deptford. It was given out (and we are still told at school) that he died in a tavern brawl; but the indication seems to be that his murderer was an accredited agent, for though his identity was known, no steps were taken against him.

Penry, yet another of the Mermaid circle, was hanged.

From these alarming events Shakespeare and his Mermaid friends learnt to be discreet. They developed ingenuity in presenting their "dangerous" doctrines in disguise. Beaumont cloaks their more serious activities with a facetious façade:

> *"What things have we seen*
> *Done at the Mermaid! Heard words that have been*
> *So nimble, and so full of subtile flame,*
> *As if that everyone from whence they came*
> *Had meant to put his whole wit in a jest*
> *And had resolved to live a fool the rest*
> *Of his dull life."*

We can picture the added spice for the charmed circle in attending, for instance, a new play of Shakespeare's to the deeper meaning of which only they held the key. When Goethe writes of his own *Faust* (in a letter to Eckerman, dated January 29, 1827): "All in *Faust* is thought out in terms of the theatre to please everyone. If the crowd of onlookers takes pleasure in its appearance, the higher meaning will not escape the observation of the initiated," he could almost be characterising the approach of the Mermaid dramatists.

These dramatists still possessed something of the swift and mobile intelligence of the best minds of the Middle Ages, which delighted in allegory and with the greatest ease followed a story on two levels of consciousness at once. Some of their work appears almost incomprehensible today, looked at purely as it stands; for they wrote in a kind of pictorial code for each other and for posterity, partly because it belonged to a Rosicrucian path to transform ideas into pictures, but also for the very practical reason that it was not safe to write more openly. Once one *has* the key, a light is shed both on Shakespeare and on the group around him. We see now why so often their meaning is hidden under pictures from Greek myths, or wrapped in symbolism, and why the purely intellectual critic is so often led astray, as in the case of Shakespeare's poem, *The Phoenix and the Turtle*, which appeared in Chester's *Love's Martyr*, along with others by Chester, Marston, Chapman and Ben Jonson on the same theme, and in which an eminent commentator, Dr. Grossart, identified the Phoenix as Elizabeth and Essex as the Turtle!

Yet Chester's preface makes it clear that the poems are concerned not with personalities but with spiritual symbols:

"You whose thoughts follow profound studies, read these reflections, formed by pure love, abandoning error. You whose darkened imagination thinks what is told here is a fable, learn more, seek more, and you will find pure truth."

For the Phoenix Mysteries of Tyre and Damar-Sheba were Mysteries of Death and Rebirth. Herodotus tells us that the Phoenix was a sacred and exceedingly rare bird, which came, once every five hundred years, from its home in Arabia to the Temple of the Sun at Heliopolis, to burn itself in a nest of spice, and out of its own ashes to rise renewed. Its fame had early reached the shores of Anglo-Saxon England; a poem in *The Book of Exeter* tells how it is born again from its own egg, hatched by the flames, and that : "after that conflagration, an apple's likeness will be found among the ashes." And it had its place in the Grail story; we read in Wolfram von Eschenbach's *Parzival*:

> *"That stone is both pure and precious;*
> *by its magic the wondrous bird,*
> *The Phoenix, becometh ashes;*
> *and yet doth such virtue flow*
> *from the stone, that afresh it riseth,*
> *renewed from the ashes' glow,*
> *and the plumes that erstwhile it moulted*
> *spring forth yet more fair and bright.*
> *…And this stone all men call the Grail."*

Similarly, in Rosicrucianism, the Phoenix was the human soul on its path of inner development. The whole of *The Chymical Wedding* is written under its sign; its story is that of the Phoenix transmuted into alchemical pictures – the rebirth of the young King and Queen into their garments of gentle crystal is a metamorphosis of the death and rebirth of the Phoenix.

In the Phoenix and the Turtle, Shakespeare stops short of this rebirth. Keats has said of him: "Nothing is true to him till he has experienced it on his own pulses." In the year this poem appeared – 1601 – what Shakespeare was experiencing on his pulses was death; he was unable to bring Hamlet to rebirth, either. Utter and complete resurrection he was indeed not to experience till when, much later, he had plumbed the abysses of still further blows of Fate.

In the next chapter we will accompany him on his initiation by life, and trace how the experiences outer circumstances brought to him were woven into his soul's history and how they fostered his flowering of the spirit.

CHAPTER IV

SHAKESPEARE'S LIFE

"In a wonderful way we see in Shake-
speare's own person what we may call a
Mystery-development intended by very
Nature".

RUDOLF STEINER[9]

WILLIAM SHAKESPEARE was born at Stratford-on-Avon on April 23rd, 1564, the third child and eldest son of John Shakespeare, a white-tawer, who made gloves, girdles, purses and parchment from the softest leathers – lambskin, deerskin, kid. For this craft great artistry and delicacy of touch were necessary. He still clung to the old faith, and, as we shall see, had the Catholics' friendliness towards the Drama. It would seem that some dramatic ability ran in the family, for his youngest son Edmund also became an actor – and one of sufficient note to be buried in Southwark Cathedral.

John Shakespeare's wife, Mary, was an Arden of Wilm-scote, a family of yeomen farmers claiming descent from Turchill, the Anglo-Saxon thane from whose defence-mounds at Warwick the great castle there later developed.

[9] SHAKESPEARE AND THE NEW IDEALS

When he bowed to the Norman custom of using a surname, he took the name of his Warwickshire forest, the Forest of Arden, a forest remembered today only in the place-name, Henley-in-Arden, and as the scene of *As You Like It*.

Stratford, then a little market-town in a quiet countryside, nourished the growing boy on sights and sounds of Nature whose unspoilt beauty, as is evident in many a felicitous descriptive passage, stayed with him all his life. "We find in his plays about a hundred and fifty names of plants and about a hundred names of birds, and everywhere intimately, lovingly, interwoven with human life." [10]

The town had a possession of great spiritual significance in its school, which Shakespeare attended till his thirteenth year. This was not one of the relatively new Grammar Schools instituted by Edward VI, but an ancient foundation from the thirteenth century, endowed by the Guild of the Holy Cross (whose Chapel still stands near it). This Guild had a certain esoteric content, for the Legend of the Holy Cross is the other half of that Temple Legend which flowed into Rosicrucianism. Many of the Guilds in Shakespeare's day were also craftsmen's Mermaids.

One can well understand that, in view of his destiny, it was important that in his childhood and adolescence Shakespeare should see and experience those medieval Mystery-Cycles which fathered his own dramas. By the sixteenth century only six of these cycles were still being annually performed in England (for three days each Corpus Christi) – the Cornish (*in* Cornish), the Norwich, the Chester, the Wakefield, the York, and the Coventry Cycles. Coventry was within easy riding distance of Stratford; his father was a Catholic; and testimony that

---

[10] Rudolf Steiner: SHAKESPEARE AND THE NEW IDEALS

Shakespeare *did* see these plays, and that they engraved themselves livingly upon his memory, is scattered through his own.

Thus, Hamlet, warning the players at Elsinore not to "tear a passion to tatters," utters the famous phrase which has become part of the English language:

> *It out-herod's Herod.*
> > *(Hamlet , III, ii)*

(In the *Three Kings Play*, Herod rants like the wildest madman). Recollections of Hell's Mouth in red-and-black activity produce the Boy's reminiscence of the dead Falstaff:

> *Do you not remember, he saw a flea stick upon*
> *Bardolph's red nose, and he said it was a black*
> *soul burning in Hell?*
> > *(Henry V, II, iii)*

The slaughter of the Innocents in the *Three Kings Play* colours Henry V's appeal to the Governors of Harfleur to surrender the city and so avoid the aftermath of siege:

> *Your naked infants spitted upon pikes,*
> *Whiles the mad mothers with their howls confus'd*
> *Do break the clouds, as did the wives of Jewry*
> *At Herod's bloody-hunting slaughtermen.*
> > *(Henry V, III, iii)*

And mad Lear's picture of woman –

> *Down from the waist they are Centaurs.*
> *Though woman all above:*
> *But to the girdle do the gods inherit;*
> *beneath it is all the fiends'*
>
>   *(Lear,* IV, vi)

slides from the Greek picture of supersensible man into
the Tempter in the *Adam and Eve Play*, who is directed
to be "a fine adder made with a virgin's face and yellow
hair upon her head."
Nor was the district devoid of elements of culture.
Coventry had its beautiful fifteenth-century Gothic cathedral, before which was the opening playing-station of the
Mystery-Cycles. At near-by Warwick, on the way to
Coventry, the Beauchamp Chapel was one of England's
most famous shrines of Gothic art. Nearer home still was
the noble castle of Kenilworth, which Shakespeare as a
child was free to roam, for his mother's kinsman, Edward
Arden, was the Earl of Leicester's trusted right-hand man.
Court revels and Royalty herself became realities when, in
1575 (Shakespeare being then eleven years old),
Elizabeth visited Kenilworth. The wind-vane instability
of the favour of the great also became a reality when, the
following year, Edward Arden was executed as a result
of the Queen's visit. Meanwhile, from the fabulous water-
show in honour of that visit, the boy's marvelling mind
had plucked a mermaid singing on a dolphin's back, to
be brought forth from its treasure-house later in *A Midsummer Night's Dream*.

In those days when every craft had its guild and hence

an acknowledged place in the established order, the spontaneous birth of the professional player placed him outside the accepted social categories; and troupes touring the countryside could be whipped out of town as rogues and vagabonds unless they could show proof that some great lord was their protector. Their first action, therefore, on arrival on any new town, was to seek out the High Bailifff and produce their credentials. If he was a Puritan, he sent them packing forthwith; if he was a Catholic, he allowed them to rehearse a play in his presence; if it passed his censorship, they had his permission to perform it publicly in one of the innyards of the town.

In 1569, John Shakespeare was High Bailiff of Stratford. A travelling troupe presented themselves and craved leave to show their paces. He was no Puritan; he gladly granted it. Tradition has it that it was then, a child five years old standing between his father's knees, that Shakespeare saw, in the Guildhall beneath the Guild Schoolroom, his first professional players rehearse his first secular play.

Between then and his departure from Stratford at the age of twenty-one, it is on record that no less than twenty-four troupes visited and played in the town. We may be fairly sure that Shakespeare saw them all play, and that during the last nine years of this period James Burbage's playhouse was often mentioned by them in his hearing.

There were three Stratford taverns at which these strolling players stayed – the Swan, the Crown and the Bear. These, it is said, Shakespeare haunted, first as boy and then as youth, whenever the players were there, fascinated by their tales and the breath they brought of the outside world. One can see him, his imagination all on fire, being helped by them to set his feet on the road to his own destiny.

Apart from these formative forces and these incisions from without, both quietly preparing him for his task, we know few concrete facts concerning his adolescence. Except that his father took him from school at the age of thirteen to help him in his business, we do not even know how he was occupied when he went about his lawful occasions; as regards his unlawful ones, the deer-stealing story offers conjectures. When he inserts in his plays a passage which has little relevance to either the character or the actions, it is not unreasonable to assume that is has some personal relevance. Such a passage occurs in the pious wish (which seems to have no connection with its context) of the Old Shepherd in *The Winter's Tale*:

> *I would there were no age between sixteen and three-and-twenty, or that youth would sleep, out the rest; for there is nothing in the between but getting wenches with child, wronging the ancientry, stealing, fighting.*
>
> *(The Winter's Tale*, III, iii)

On November 27th, 1582, the Bishop of Worcester's Register issued a special licence for the marriage of William Shakespeare and Anne Whately, both eighteen years of age. Next day a marriage Bond was posted, exempting the Bishop of Worcester from all responsibility should the marriage of William Shakespeare and Anne Hathaway not prove valid because of some previous contract of either party. Shakespeare being a minor, two sureties stood for him – Fulk Sandells and John Richardson, farmers, formerly friends of Richard Hathaway, Anne's father, who had died the previous year. This marriage took place without delay. The bride's age was twenty-six.

Shakespeare brought his wife to live in his father's house; less than six months later, their first child, Susanna, was born. Shakespeare's youngest brother, Edmund (who later followed him to London and became an actor) was then only three years old, so little uncle and little niece were brought up together like brother and sister.

Two years later, in 1585, Shakespeare's twins, Judith and Hamnet, were born. In that same year Shakespeare leaving his family in his parents care, left Stratford and went to London.

What external circumstance was the catalyst that precipitated this departure we do not know. Home-life must have had its tensions; for while on the one hand his father was a Catholic; Anne was a Puritan, so that Shakespeare lived with two extremes between which, as a man of his age, he sought to tread the middle way.

Puritanism, moreover, had set its face against the plays and play-acting, which Shakespeare, with each visit of the players, must have realised more deeply belonged to his own world. In that year (1585) two troupes had visited Stratford; one of these, the Earl of Leicester's Men, included Richard Burbage, later to become the greatest of Elizabethan actors and Shakespeare's co-"housekeeper". He was the son of that same James Burbage who had built the first English playhouse nine years earlier; and as it was to James Burbage that Shakespeare presented himself immediately on his arrival in London, it does not seem unreasonable to suppose that he was following Richard Burbage's advice. It could well have been this advice which led to Shakespeare's departure, or perhaps a quarrel with Anne rising from it. For there is the ring of first-hand experience in such passages as the following:

> *So that this land, like an offensive wife*
> *That has enraged him on to offer strokes,*
> *As he is striking, holds his infant up,*
> *And hangs resolved correction in the arm*
> *That was upreared to execution.*
>
> *(Henry IV, Part II, IV, i)*

Characters in his plays voice over and over again the warning that a man should not marry a woman older than himself; and in *The Comedy of Errors*, an early play which has otherwise little characterisation, we get a vigorous and clearcut portrait of Adriana, a wife older than her husband, whose character as a jealous shrew is strongly emphasised. In an otherwise light-hearted dialogue, the husband exclaims:

> *She that doth call me husband, even my soul*
> *Doth for my wife abhor.*
>
> *(The Comedy of Errors, III, ii)*

Whatever the precipitating circumstance, the underlying facts were that Shakespeare had reached the age of twenty-one, when the ego incarnates, and that the wings of young genius were growing and driving him to use them. One feels that Anne must often have had occasion to accuse him, as Anthony à Wood was later to accuse John Aubrey, of being "roving and magotie-headed".

It is significant that it is in his earlier work, when the personal experience of being "cribb'd, cabin'd and confin'd" by his small Stratford world is still fresh in him,that he writes such passages as:

> *Homekeeping youths have ever homely wits.*
> *I rather would entreat thy company*
> *To see the wonders of the world abroad,*
> *Than, living dully sluggardis'd at home,*
> *Wear out thy youth with shapeless idleness.*
>
> *(Two Gentlemen of Verona, I, i)*

Or as this:

> *Such wind as scatters young men through the world,*
> *To seek their fortune further than at home,*
> *Where small experience grows.*
>
> *(The Taming of the Shrew, I, ii)*

The journey to London on horseback took three days, with two nights spent at Oxford and Woodstock, at the taverns at which Shakespeare continued to break his journey on his yearly visits to his family at Straford. The tavern at Oxford was the Crown, where his hostess, Mistress Davenant, "used much to delight in his pleasant company". Shakespeare was later to be godfather to her son, born in 1606, who was to become Sir William Davenant, Poet Laureate and a playwright of some note, and who bore so marked a resemblance to his godfather, both in features and in literary gifts, that he was widely regarded as his son.

It is from this same Sir William Davenant that we hear that, on arrival in London, Shakespeare sold his horse at Smithfield to James Burbage, who kept a livery stable there in connection with his playhouse, The Theatre,

outside which Shakespeare began life in London as a
horse-boy in charge of playgoers' horses. Presently, he
found his way within, first as "servitor" to the actors
("one who attendedth the players at their plays and goeth
abroad on errands"); then as "prompter's attendant"
(call-boy); then as "hireling actor", as which he received
a salary of six and eightpence a week.

To become even a "hireling actor" called for some training. Tarleton, the first great star of the Elizabethan stage,
"who for the part called the Clown's part never had his
match", was a shareholding actor – known as a "housekeeper" – in Burbage's company, now The Lord Chamberlain's Men. He was a patient and painstaking teacher
of young actors, who, for the playing-in-the-round of the
Elizabethan open stage, needed to be coached in skilful
"turning". To Tarleton Shakespeare owed that sympa-
thetic grooming which led him from beneath the stage to
on to it.

To Tarleton Shakespeare, indeed, owed infinitely more.
At crucial moments in our lives the right souls come to
meet us. At this crucial moment in Shakespeare's, Tarleton was such a soul.

Such was Tarleton's whimsicality that his expression
alone could cause a riot as his head came up through a
stage trap-door:

> "Tarleton, when his head alone was seen,
> The tire-house door and tapistrie between,
> Set all the multitude in such a laughter,
> They could not hold for scarce an hour after."

Yet such was the harmony of his own feeling-life that it

was always he who was called upon to *quell* the riot when the groundlings got out of hand:
"And let Tarleton entreat the young people of the city either to abstain altogether from plays or to use themselves after a more quiet order."
So amiable was his character, and so full of humanity his fooling, that his famous russet coat was hailed with affection by simple and sophisticated alike. Before he had been an actor he had been one the Elizabeth's jesters, and it is recorded that "he told the Queen more home-truths than all her chaplains, and cured her melancholy better than all her physicians". It was Tarleton's David-harp that Shakespeare essayed to place in the hands of all his Fools. There were qualities in Tarleton which passed as seed into Shakespeare's being, to come to a different birth as the latter's development unfolded. He lived just long enough to do what he had to do for Shakespeare; he died in 1588.

To his role of hireling actor, Shakespeare now added that of "play-furbisher", the hack-writer who polished up old plays. And from that he graduated to the writing of plays in his own right, and so became the Theatre's only dramatist.
By the time he was twenty-eight – within seven years of his arrival – he had made a place and a name for himself in the world of the theatre; but not without arousing jealousy. Before his meteoric descent on that world, Marlowe, Greene, Nash and Peele had supplied Burbage with his plays; and Shakespeare, coming as a novice to this new craft of play-writing, had modelled, in his first attempts, his style on theirs.
As Greene lay dying, in great poverty, he addressed to Marlowe, Nashe and Peele a pamphlet entitled, *A Groats-*

worth of Wit Bought with a Million of Repentance. In this he warns them of the ingratitude of the actors, who now turn to another playwright, and darts a barb at Shakespeare as that playwright:

"Base-minded men all three of you, if by my misery you be not warned; for unto none of you, like me, sought those burrs to cleave; those puppets, I mean, that speak from our mouths … Yea, trust them not, for there is an upstart crow, beautified with our feathers, that, with his tiger's heart wrapped in a player's hide, supposes he is as well able to bombast out a blank verse as the best of you; and, being an absolute Johannes Factotum, is in his own conceit the only Shake-scene in a country."

Henry Cheetle, the publisher, brought out this pamphlet in a hurry in August, 1592, immediately following Greene's death. In December of the same year, in his own book, *Kindhearts's Dream*, he makes Shakespeare this handsome apology:

"I am as sorry as if the original fault had been my fault, because myself have seen his demeanour no less civil than he excellent in the quality he professes. Besides, divers of worship have reported his uprightness of dealing, which argues his honesty, and his facetious grace in writing, that approves his art."

For though, in Shakespeare's early days in London, he doubtless frequented the humbler taverns, and came to know the Bardolphs and Pyms to whom he afterwards gave immortality, he was by now already mixing on terms of some intimacy with the young courtiers who frequented the theatre and the Mermaid, in spite of the fact that, as a member of the Lord Chamberlain's Men, he wore Lord Hunsdon's livery; and when, in the following year (1593, his eighth in London), his childhood's friends, Richard Field, printed his first major poem, *Venus and Adonis*, it was dedicated to the twenty-year-old Earl of Southampton, and was received with great acclaim by the young nobles of the court.

The Puritan Lord Mayor and Aldermen of London had tried in very way they could think of to drive the play-houses outside the City limits; but their efforts had so far been foiled by the Lord Chamberlain, who was the actors' very good friend. But now, in this same year in which the Puritan City Fathers launched their bolts against the Mermaid, the Plague broke out in London, and, the death rate having reached the prescribed thirty a week, the City's three playhouses – The Theatre, The Curtain and The Rose – were compulsorily closed, and the players went on tour in rural England.

These months on tour must have been for Shakespeare a time of trial. He was familiar with the idea of tests and trials of the soul in the Mysteries and the myths and in Rosicrucianism, and had already used it, a little falter-ingly, in *Love's Labour's Lost*; but when one is young it is not so easy to bear tests and trials of one's own soul like a Christian.

As a boy he had thrilled to the arrival of the players in their two great ship-like wagons, gorgeously painted in crimson and gold, each drawn by six horses, trumpets blowing, drums beating. (A record of such an arrival in Stourbridge in 1610 runs: "The players, with their apparel, drums and trumpets, carts and wagons, came *sounding* to their inn.") But, again, to be one of the players oneself was quite a different matter, playing on the improvised pageant-stage in country innyards, or, in wet weather, in barns. (In 1607 Dekker makes fun of the players on tour "for driving the poor country people to sit cackling in old barns.")

Nor would the rustic audiences help his self-esteem by
their vociferous preference for the old plays, and these
unfurbished. Shakespeare, in London the rising poet-
dramatist, the acknowledged genius, on tour falls to the
estate of the almost-a-vagabond strolling player.

In 1594 the Plague subsided; the players returned to
London; The Theatre opened again; *The Rape of Lucrece*,
again dedicated to Southampton, was published and
found favour; Southampton himself, on coming of age,
gave Shakespeare a gift of (according to Sir William
Davenant) £1,000; at Christmas, together with his Company's star actors, Richard Burbage and William Kempe,
Shakespeare played in two comedies before the Queen at
Court. This particular bad time was over.

Southampton's munificence made it possible for Shakespeare to graduate from hireling to share-holding actor
in Burbage's playhouse. These "housekeepers" were
something much more than mere business or professional
associates. They were in a real sense a community (in
this case, a community of seven); their working together
was a deed of communal creation. As one share-holding
player died, his place was taken by another, but the
groups went on as an inwardly living entity. For the next
nineteen years –till in 1613 he retired to Stratford at the
age of forty-nine – Shakespeare remained an integral
part of this close-knit working community. In his Will
he refers warmly to members of it as "my comrades".

He was to find that being a housekeeper could involve
one in unexpected and sometimes unorthodox activities.
With an eye to an audience drawn from courtiers, law
students and solid citizens, James Burbage had built The
Theatre on the North bank of the Thames, on a pleasant
site amid open spaces, little hills with windmills on them,
archery grounds, "divers fair houses for merchants, and

many fair summer-houses for refreshment," with the Temple not far away, and beyond that, Greenwich Palace, when the Queen and her Court were frequently in residence. The site was leased for twenty-one years. In 1597, when the lease was running out, the owner of the land refused renewal.

The housekeepers looked around for a new site, and bought a plot of land on the South side of the river, among low taverns, bear-pits and houses of ill-repute, where the narrow streets were always full of shouting, jostling crowds,and the air often smelt of bears, and where, when the famous bear Sackerton got loose, as he had a habit of doing, confusion was worse confounded, as Shakespeare so beguilingly describes:

> SLENDER: *You are afraid if you see the bear loose,*
> *are you not?*
> ANNE: *Ay, indeed, sir.*
> SLENDER: *That's meat and drink to me now. I have*
> *seen Sackerton loose twenty times and I have*
> *taken him by the chain; but I warrant you,*
> *the women have so cried and shrieked at it,*
> *that it passed; but women, indeed, cannot*
> *abide 'em; they are very ill-favoured*
> *rough things.*
>
> *(The Merry Wives of Windsor, I, i)*

James Burbage had just died; but his wife and her two sons, with Shakespeare and the other members of the company, "did come on a riotous manner, with swords and carpenter's tools". They pulled down the wooden theatre, loaded all the planks and beams on to carts, and took the dismantled playhouse across London Bridge, past the skulls of traitors bleaching on their poles, to its new home near Sackerton's. Here they put the playhouse together again and gave it a new name – The Globe. And here Shakespeare's plays continued to appear and he to work till the translated playhouse was burned down in 1613.

At the same time as the rebuilding of the playhouse, more rebuilding (presumably in a less riotous manner) was going forward in Stratford, where Shakespeare had bought, and was now repairing for his family, the second largest house, New Place. His cogitations over this, revealing the poet's practical business side, appear in a passage in *Henry IV, Part II*, on which he was concurrently engaged:

> *When we mean to build,*
> *We first survey the plot, then draw the model;*
> *Then we must rate the cost of erection,*
> *Question surveyors, know our own estate,*
> *How able such a work to undergo –*
>
> *(Henry IV Part II, I, iii)*

It is an engaging detail that, after carrying out extensive alterations, Shakespeare had a ton of stone left over, which he sold to the Corporation for tenpence, for the repair of Clopton Bridge.

At about the same time an appeal for a coat of arms is granted. From now on, Shakespeare can – and does – sign himself, *Gentleman*; yet this does not prevent the onlooker in him making fun of it all, as when Slender says of his cousin Shallow:

> *A gentleman born, who writes himself* Armerigo*;*
> *in any bill, warrant, quittance, or obligation,*
> Armerigo. *All his successors, gone before him,*
> *have done it; and all his ancestors, that come after*
> *him, may.*
>
> (The Merry Wives of Windsor, I, i)

By 1598 Shakespeare is acknowledged as the writer of greatest stature among Elizabethan dramatists. Francis Meres reports in his *Paladis Tamia*, published in that year:
"As Plautus and Seneca are accounted the best for Comedy and Tragedy among the Latins, so Shakespeare among the English is the most excellent in both kinds for the stage."
And yet Shakespeare was at that time only beginning to unfold his more serious dramatic powers, particularly in the portrayal of the individual human being. In 1596 his eleven-year-old son Hamnet had died, and one can often trace in a creative artist a deepening of imaginative power following the death of someone with close connections (as in Da Vinci, for example, after the death of his father). Blake himself records his own awareness of an enrichment of inspiration received in this way following the death of his younger brother. In the case of Shakespeare, two other great strides forward follow two further deaths – his father's death in 1601 ushers in his period of great tragedies, and in the three romances which follow his mother's death in 1608 there is a flowering of that Mystery-content which had first tentatively budded in *Pericles* earlier in that same year.

Such influences steal into a man's soul-history in silence and stillness, dropping like the gentle dew from heaven; but during the years between his son's death and his father's there were other influences which erupted tempestuously into Shakespeare's life.

Endless controversy has raged round the mystery of who was the "dark lady" and who the "lovely boy" of Shakespeare's sonnets. But the sonnets record how for the lovely boy he conceived an ardent friendship, and for the dark lady a love which became a "maddening fever". He was an actor, they were nobly born; when the lovely boy began to act as a link between them, the dark lady – "for thou art covetous and he is kind" (*Sonnet CXXXIV*) – quickly had him, also, in thrall.

That already in 1599 Shakespeare was aware of their betrayal, yet still hoped against hope for a happy issue, is clear from *Sonnet CXLIV*, which was piratically published that year in *The Passionate Pilgrim*:

> *Two loves I have of comfort and despair,*
> *Which like two spirits do suggest me still:*
> *The better angel is a man right fair,*
> *The worser spirit a woman colour'd ill.*
> *To win me soon to hell, my female evil*
> *Tempteth my better angel from my side,*
> *And would corrupt my saint to be a devil,*
> *Wooing his purity with her foul pride.*
> *And whether my angel be turn'd fiend*
> *Suspect I may, yet not directly tell;*
> *But being both from me, both to each friend,*
> *I guess one angel in another's hell:*
> > *Yet this shall I ne'er know, but live in doubt,*
> > *Till my bad angel fire my good one out.*

But this happy issue failed to materialize. As late as 1607, *Antony and Cleopatra* reveals traces of her witchery still lurking in his blood.

All the passions of those tumultuous years storm through the Sonnets – agony, ecstacy, complaint, complaisance, humiliation, estrangement, reconciliation, even renunciation:

> *Take all my loves, my love, yea, take them all …*
> *I do forgive thy robbery, gentle thief,*
> *Although thou steal thee all my poverty;*
> *And yet love knows it is a greater grief*
> *To bear love's wrong than hate's known injury.*
>
> *(Sonnet XL)*

Shakespeare has been jettisoned out of himself:

> *Beshrew that heart that makes my heart to groan*
> *For that deep wound it gives my friend and me!*
> *Is't not enough to torture me alone,*
> *But slave to slavery my sweet'st friend must be?*
> *Me from myself thy cruel eye hath taken,*
> *And my next self thou harder hast engross'd:*
> *Of him, myself and thee I am forsaken;*
> *A torment thrice threefold thus to be cross'd.*
>
> *(Sonnet CXXXIII)*

But when the torment thrice threefold is over, he comes back to himself with heightened self-awareness. Now he is able to portray in Hamlet an ego not yet held secure and self-contained and self-possessed by a firm central point within.

"These", say Goethe, "are no mere poems. It is as
though the great leaves of Fate were opened and the
stormwind of life were blowing through them, turning
them quickly to and fro." Looking back later, we can
see how this stormwind blessed Shakespeare while it
buffeted him, developing in him that sensitive inwardness out of which he wrote his series of great tragedies,
each one more heartrending than the last, and opening
his soul to a plumbing of tragic experience which was
in key with the outer events which now darkened the
national horizon.

For as within, so without; the gloom of Elizabethan
London from the turn of the century matched his own.
A startling mood of pessimism is revealed in some writers
of the time, a counterpart of Hamlet's description of man
as "a quintessence of dust". The Queen was ageing, sick,
and lonely and of uncertain temper. The Court was no
longer a gay and brilliant place, but filled with tension
and uncertainty. Who would succeed her? No-one knew.
The Earl of Essex, an immensely popular hero, made
approaches to James of Scotland and tried to stir up the
disaffected in London against the Queen. In 1601, his
abortive attempt was crushed. His execution followed.
His friend and kinsman, Southampton, who had supported him, was also sentenced to death, but instead was
imprisoned in the Tower, where he remained till James
I's accession released him.
Both these noblemen were friends of Shakespeare's.
Their downfall filled him with bitterness against the
Queen. Even after her death, when asked to write a poem
in her honour, he refused.
To add to all this, the housekeepers of the Globe had,
in connection with this abortive rebellion, a burden

of anxiety peculiarly their own. Sir William Percy, a sup-
porter of Essex, had asked them to put on a production
of *Richard II*, implementing his request with a gift of
forty shillings. They had done so in all innocence. But it
was timed, without their knowledge, to coincide with
Essex's entry of London, in the hope that it would rouse
the populace to revolt. An enquiry by the privy Council
later absolved The Globe of guilt: but only after some
delay, and in the meantime no-one knew what the
verdict might be or what extreme penalties might yet be
imposed.

A mist of elusiveness enwraps Shakespeare the man; his
plays are written, as Ariel's invisible music was played,
by a picture of Nobody. We know less about his daily
human life than we do, for example, about Chaucer's.
We have a bright endearing miniature in our minds of
Chaucer, when his day's work as Comptroller of Customs
and Subsidies is over, retreating to his tower above
Aldgate, one of London's medieval gatehouses, and
sitting at his bookes and his devotioun until he blissfully
makes ful oft his head to ache. But where, in a London
of 300,000 inhabitants (of whom one in every five hundred is, like himself, busy writing a play), does Shakespeare mull over North's Plutarch's *Lives*, or Ovid's
Metamorphoses, or Montaigne's essay, *Of the Caniballes*,
which inspired Gonzalo's commonwealth?
So it is corn in Egypt to our famished fantasy when,
through some such eyelet window as the Belott Suit, we
get a glimpse of Shakespeare in a domestic setting.
This suit was brought in 1612 by Belott, a London
Huguenot, against his father-in-law, Christopher Mountjoy, a tire-maker (a maker of women's head-dresses),
also a London Huguenot. Belott is married to Christo-

pher's daughter Mary, and Christopher had promised
that with her should come a dowry of £60; but though
the marriage took place some years ago, the dowry has
not been paid. Joan Johnson, Christopher's maidservant,
deposes that from 1602 to 1604 Shakespeare was lodging
with the tire-maker and that at the latter's request he
had joined him in persuading Belott to agree to the
match. Shakespeare, questioned, praises Belott's character. He remembers discussion of the dowry, but not the sum
agreed upon. The case being referred to the Overseers of
the Huguenot Church in London, they direct that
Christopher, should now pay his son-in-law a belated
dowry of twenty nobles.

How comforting, one feels, it must have been to Shakespeare to be able, amid the storm and stress of writing
Hamlet and *Othello*, to relax among homely people, and
talk mundane talk of dowries, and be witty at the
expense of the latest women's head-dress!

In 1603, within ten days of James I's arrival in London,
he had issued a Royal Warrant appointing The Globe's
players to be known as the King's Men. It was in itself
an honour, but it brought in its train an indignity hard for
sensitive genius to bear. Each player was issued with four
and a half yards of red cloth; and when, in the following
year, the King made his formal entry into London, they
walked in procession through the city, wearing his livery
of a scarlet cloak bearing his arms, like and with his other
servants. It was a mere straw compared with Shakespeare's
other burdens; but it must have seemed to him a last straw.
To have the Mountjoy household to go home to must
have been a boon to his tense nerves.

Already the Sonnet stormwind is sowing seed. The

purged soul has opened to receive compassion.In tragedies by Shakespeare's contemporaries, such as Webster's
Duchess of Malfi, horror is piled upon horror, without
stirring commensurate pity; but now in *King Lear*, Shakespeare's catharsis through suffering really does lead
through in a quite new way, a modern way, to pity and
compassion, both in the play's characters and in ourselves.

Pericles sounds a new note, *Hamlet*, *King Lear*, *Timon of
Athens* all had been unable to go beyond death; now
some barrier is down, and Shakespeare goes forward
through death to resurrection. Between *Pericles* and the
three later plays of this last group intervene two blows
of fate – his mother's death in 1608 (of which we have
already spoken), and in 1609 the unauthorised publication of his entire Sonnet-sequence, laying bare before the
eyes of the world all the innermost intimacies and
agonies, the anguish of soul and spirit, of that stormwind
period. But it is as if through these fresh fires Shakespeare
passes unscathed and only more finely tempered. The
"gold button on the bough" of *Pericles* comes to full
flower in *The Tempest*.

What has happened to Shakespeare is nothing less than
the miracle of rebirth in *The Chymical Wedding* taking
place in his own being. He has written the end of the *The
Phoenix and the Turtle* into the script of his own soul-
history. It is to this great Mystery-experience that he
struggles to give expression in this last group of plays, at
first haltingly, at last with soaring certainty.

On June 29th, 1613, The Globe was staging a spectacular
first performance of *Henry VIII*, a new play to which
Shakespeare is believed to have contributed the Queen
Katharine scenes. "King Henry making a masque at
Cardinal Wolsey's House, and certain cannons being

shot off at his entry, some of the Paper wherewith one of
them was stopped did light on the Thatch, where, being
thought at first but an idle smoak, and their eyes more
attentive to the show, it kindled inwardly and ran round
like a train, consuming in less than an hour the whole
House to the very ground." [11]
There was no loss of life; playgoers' breeches which had
caught fire were, with great presence of mind, put out
with tankards of ale. But all the company's stock of
costumes and properties went up in flames, and the
fabulous financial loss this entailed is indicated by the
records, in the contemporary *Henslowe Diary*, of expendi-
ture at the Rose Theatre, where one stage-cloak alone
cost a quarter of what Shakespeare had paid for the
second largest house in Stratford, with two gardens and
two orchards. (Spenser takes this magnificence for
granted:

"Yclad in costly garments fit for tragic Stage."

And Wooton, in the letter just quoted, speaks of the play
concerned being "set forth with pomp and majesty, the
Knights of the Order with their Georges and Garter, the
guards with their embroidered coats and the like.")
Worse still, from posterity's point of view, was the
perishing of numerous play scripts. We shall never know
how many precious dramas of the period were lost to us
in this way, though there is a tradition that while The
Globe was burning, and its audience of between two and
three thousand were elbowing their escape, one of the
actors rushed back into danger to rescue what prompt
books he could, and that among what he retrieved were

[11] Sir William Wootton, Letter to his nephews, July 2nd, 1613

those original Shakespeare drafts from which the First Folio was later to be completed.

For twenty-eight years, ever since he arrived in London, first as The Theatre in Finsbury Fields, then as The Globe at Bankside, this playhouse had been the scene of Shakespeare's labours. Ever since he had become one of its housekeepers and had in a riotous manner helped to transport it across the river and re-erect it cosily close to the Bear-Garden, he had been its popularity's chief architect, that father of its fortunes; it was with his own life-forces that he had nourished its fame. Now, as he saw the flames leap upwards, to shrivel the flag which proclaimed to the playgoing public that this was a playing-day, and to engulf the lofty hut from which Jupiter would never again descend on *Cymbeline* nor Juno in *The Winter's Tale*; as he saw the flames dart downwards to lick the golden stars from heaven's curtains and sweep through the property dock from which Desdemona's bed would never again be rolled, can we doubt that something in Shakespeare's life-organism died?

The Globe, like Prospero's greater globe, had melted into air, into thin air; and Shakespeare that same year retired to Stratford. In 1614 the new Globe, reported to be "the fairest theatre in England", was opened on the same site; here it stood for another thirty years, till, during the Civil War, the Puritans pulled it down. But Shakespeare wrote nothing for it; within two years he himself had passed away.

On February 10th, 1616, Shakespeare's youngest daughter Judith was married to Thomas Quiney, the son of her father's life-long friend who in their schooldays had been the boy next door. Drayton and Ben Jonson came to the wedding .It would seem that their convivial company proved too much for what one cannot but think had

since the burning of The Globe been a failing body and
diminishing life-forces; Shakespeare "fell ill of a feavour",
and died on his fifty-second birthday, April 23rd, 1616.
He was buried in the chancel of Stratford parish church
beneath a disconcerting epitaph said to have been composed by himself:

> *"Good friend, for Jesu's sake forbear*
> *To dig the dust enclosed here.*
> *Blessed be the man that spares these stones,*
> *And cursed be he that moves my bones."*

Was it this epitaph, one wonders, which moved Miss
Delia Bacon to second thoughts when, in 1856, she
descended on Stratford from America, demanding permission (which, astonishingly, she received) to search
this grave for papers? Has it played a part in protecting
Shakespeare's remains from removal to Westminster
Abbey? It belongs to his soul's history that it was on
St. George's Day, the day of England's patron saint (that
is, her spiritual leader), that he both was born and died.
It would seem also to belong to that soul's history that
his chrysalis should remain were he both entered it and
left it – at the very heart of England.

CHAPTER V

SHAKESPEARE'S
WORLD OF PICTURES

"The greatest thing by far is to be a
master of metaphor. It is the sign of
original genius, and implies intuitive perception".

ARISTOTLE

WE have spoken of Shakespeare as one
of those messengers of destiny whose
task it was to lead the English people
into the modern age. Lord Bacon had
a similar task. But whereas the trend
of his essays and scientific works was
to direct men towards the modern materialistic outlook
and to prepare them for their present mastery over
Nature, Shakespeare's plays were intended to guide them
through and beyond this to a rediscovery of the Spirit
behind matter.

Hc himself does (as we have seen) experience in his own
life, both outer and inner, the distraints and desolations
of the soul travelling this path; and (as we shall see)
these he does depict in a corresponding sequence of his
plays.Yet the poet in him is able to feel on his pulses
these reverberations of the future while still living within

the world of pictures bequeathed by the Middle Ages to
his own.

His picture of the theatre, for example, along with that
of Elizabethans in general, remains to the end, despite
the shattering impact of Copernicus, completely Ptolemaic.

This is implicit in his description of The Curtain playhouse as "this wooden O", and of the Globe Theatre as
"this thronged round, this fair-filled globe." It is clearly
formulated when he says:

> *"The earth's a stage to heaven's surrounding eye,*
> *For men to act their parts."*

And Poole formulates it even more clearly:

> *"So then the world a theatre doth present,*
> *As by its roundness it appears most fit,*
> *Built with star-galleries of high ascent,*
> *In which Jehovah doth spectator sit."*

Though Copernicus has turned the universe upside
down, that reflection of it which is the Elizabethan
playhouse continues to remain true to an earlier cos-
mology, with the earth still the centre of the universe, a
planet ringed with celestial onlookers, and on it Man,
still a concern of the watchful spiritual worlds.

Though, in the state, the old World-Order may be
tottering, the playhouse still presents it in a living

tableau. In the pit stand the penny stinkards, the nut-cracking apprentices and artisans, in their flat caps, black smocks and goatskin breeches. In the circular tiers of galleries of Twopenny Rooms sit the weightier burgesses and the lesser quality, in their decent gowns and mantles. On stools on the stage, smoking Drake's new-fangled tobacco, sit the young exquisites and fops, each clothed in the cost of a farm invested in satin hose and brocade tunic. Above is the Lords' Room, giving the groundling double value for his penny, presenting to his view the grandest of the courtiers, men of nobility and notability, men who defeated the Armada, who have sailed unknown seas, who are the powers behind the Throne. In this room, it is rumoured, at private per-formances there can even be seen the Throne itself.

When Elizabeth abandoned her peripatetics between her six palaces and settled down at Westminster, her courtiers began to have Town houses and to live in London, and regular play-going became the fashion in Court circles. A new sort of playhouse was built to meet the new need – smaller, more intimate, rectangular. The round playhouse was a daylight theatre, and partly open to the weather; the new rectangular one, being roofed, could also be used by artificial light. It was, in fact, a concrete picture of modern man's freeing of himself from Nature's rhythms, and of his coming more completely into the physical body, closing the door of the fontanel after him, and shutting out the forces streaming in from the open sky.

The Blackfriars Theatre, a new little playhouse of this sort, was acquired by Shakespeare and his co-house-keepers. In the summer they gave their plays in the round "public" Globe; in the winter, in the rectangular "private" Blackfriars. They used, in fact, three metamorphoses of the theatre concurrently, for they also took up their winter quarters in the Cross Keys (whose inn-yard had been James Burbage's improvised playhouse before he built The Theatre), and used its temporary open-air pageant-stage for rehearsals of their Christmas productions at Court.

Yet these new rectangular theatres were still round in the sense that the stage, like that of the Mystery Cycles, still lay in the midst of the audience. The play was still *played* in the round; the stage was still circled round with the wonder of all eyes.

Already in Shakespeare's lifetime an attempt was made to bring in the next step in the theatre's development before its time was ripe. When King James visited Oxford in 1605, Inigo Jones experimented with the new Italianate stage placed at one end of the hall. Since this could be viewed only from the front (our front), the King and his courtiers had to evacuate the Lords' Room and head the audience, much to the discontent of the latter, who complained that now they could see only the royal back, or, at most, "one cheek only." When the King obligingly moved to the back row, so that, by turning their *backs* to the stage, they could see more of him, *they* complained that now they could not see the play, and *he* that he could not hear it. Ptolemy won; the experiment was hastily dropped and not repeated.

It was, in fact, to be another fifty-six years before this change from the native plastic pageant-stage, with the play played in the round, to the Italian operatic picture-stage, with the play played in flat profile, would be a true expression of contemporary English consciousness. By 1596 the Dutch already had it; but in England it did not arrive to stay until 1661 – the Restoration.

When the change-over *did* come – when it could be said

"With what strange ease a play may now be writ,
When the best half's composed by painting it!" –

it was Sir William Davenant, Shakespeare's godson and reputed son, who introduced it. As early as 1630, when only twenty-four years old, he had already become a leading dramatist, and for years had been writing plays-to-be-played-in-the-round for the Ptolemaic stages of Shakespeare's old theatres, the second Globe and the Blackfriars. Now, with his opera. *The Siege of Rhodes*, "illustrated by painted history represented in instantaneously changing scenes," he brought the English theatre out of Shakespeare's realm of free imagination, carrying it one step deeper into matter, one step further away from its distant source in the Mysteries.

Shakespeare's pictures of the *stage* for which he created his plays was also the picture bequeathed by the Middle Ages. For his genius and for the task assigned to it the pageant-stage proved a perfect instrument. It was a perfect symbolic arena for dramatic conflict, its opposing end-houses giving an already traditional form and pattern to his studies of the ever-changing battle between Good and Evil with Man as the battlefield, or of the deeds and sufferings of the soul on its path of inner development.

It is not often that Shakespeare used this traditional form and pattern as literally as, for example, Marlowe does in *Dr. Faustus*, when Mephistopheles, conjured up by Faustus, emerges from below, through the trap-door of Hell's Mouth, or when, crying, "Ugly Hell, gape not!," Faustus is carried alive to it. But to the Elizabethan audience, to whom the formal symbolism of the pageant-

stage was as much a part of its inherited world-picture as
it was of his, Shakespeare's mere disposition of his
characters on that stage already told them volumes.

Thus, for example, in *Richard III*, it is Richard the
murderer who, the night before Bosworth field, sleeps
before Hell's Mouth; and it is Richmond, God's
champion, who sleeps under Heaven's Tower. When the
ghosts of the murdered rise up between the two tents
through the central "grave" trapdoor, saying to the one
sleeper, "Despair and die!" and to the other, "Live and
flourish!", all is in artistic accordance with these
sleepers' locations to left and right.

In this context, stage instructions such as "Above", "On
the Walls," "At the Upper Window," "On the Balcony,"
must originally have carried deeper implications than
we are today aware of; but re-reading the plays with the
pageant-stage in mind, one realises at least what a much
freer field for quick-changing action it afforded than our
own, and how a long succession of short, sharp scenes
such as one finds, for example, in *Henry V*, could sting
the understanding into alertness with its volleys of moral
innuendo according to the side of the stage from which
they came.

Had Shakespeare died at the age of twenty-nine, as
Marlowe did, Marlowe would have been adjudged the
greater. Many aspects of Shakespeare's early work
betray a prentice hand; play by play we can watch his
gathering to a greatness. One such aspect is his characterisation.

Thus, in *Love's Labour's Lost* (1593) the characters are
silhouettes; in *Richard II* (1595) this last king belonging
to the World-Order is as stylised as a figure in a tapestry.
But "from about 1598 onwards, a certain inner life is

awakened in Shakespeare; his own artistic imagination is awakened; he is able to stamp upon his characters the very inmost of his being."[12]

How his inner pictures of his characters are from now on quickened into true imaginations we see when we compare these now living, breathing human beings with the dry bones of their sources.

Thus Plutarch writes:

"Afterwards, when Caesar's body was brought into the market-place, Antonius, making his funeral oration in praise of the dead, according to the ancient custom of Rome, and perceiving that his words moved the common people to compassion, framed his eloquence to make their hearts yearn the more."[13]

This passage Shakespeare magnificently "translates" in *Julius Caesar* into Mark Antony's famous speech:

Friends, Romans, Countrymen, lend me your ears;
I come to bury Caesar, not to praise him.
The evil that men do lives after them;
The good is oft interred with their bones.
So let it be with Caesar. The noble Brutus
Hath told you, Caesar was ambitious.
If it were so, it was a grievous fault,
And grievously hath Caesar answered it.
Here, under leave of Brutus and the rest
(For Brutus is an honourable man –
So are they all, all honourable men),
Come I to speak in Caesar's funeral.
He was my friend, faithful and just to me.
But Brutus says he was ambitious;
And Brutus is an honourable man …

(Julius Caesar, III, ii)

[12] Rudolf Steiner: SHAKESPEARE AND THE NEW IDEALS
[13] North's Plutarch's LIVES, 1575, Shakespeare's source-book also for ANTONY AND CLEOPATRA, TIMON OF ATHENS and CORIOLANUS

Plutarch goes on:
"To conclude his oration, he unfolded before the
assembly the bloody garments of the dead, thrust through
in many places with their swords, and called the male-
factors cruel and cursed murderers."
This Shakespeare transfigures into:

If you have tears, prepare to shed them now.
You all do know this mantle: I remember
The first time Caesar ever put it on;
'Twas on a summer's evening in his tent,
That day he overcame the Nervii.
Look! In this place ran Cassius' dagger through:
See what a rent the envious Casca made:
Through this, the well-belovèd Brutus stabb'd;
And as he pluck'd his cursèd steel away,
Mark how the blood of Caesar follow'd it,
As rushing out of doors, to be resolv'd
If Brutus so unkindly knock'd or no;
For Brutus, as you know, was Caesar's angel:
Judge, O you gods! how dearly Caesar lov'd him.
This was the most unkindest cut of all;
For when the mighty Caesar saw him stab,
Ingratitude, more strong that traitors' arms,
Quite vanquish'd him. Then burst his mighty heart;
And, in his mantle muffling up his face,
Even at the foot of Pompey's statue,
Which all the time ran blood, great Caesar fell.
O! what a fall was there, my countrymen.
Then I, and you, and all of us fell down.
Whilst bloody treason flourish'd over us.
O! now you weep, and I perceive you feel
The dint of pity; these are gracious drops.

Kind souls, what! weep you when you but behold
Our Caesar's vesture wounded? Look you here,
Here is himself, marr'd, as you see, with traitors.

(Julius Caesar, III, ii)

The Baconian aspect of the great change taking place in the consciousness of Western man led to a new emphasis on utility, as opposed to the previous emphasis on beauty, in his work in material substance; he was now to come to grips with the realm of matter, cut off, as we have seen, from the cosmos of which he had formerly felt himself a part.

This resulted, in the first instance, in a great impoverishment, an emptiness of soul, which has continued, alongside brilliant outer achievements, right down to our own day.

The richer realm of spiritual reality which had still been accessible to the Middle Ages by virtue of the artistic nature of their handiwork and the creative fantasy of the legends and parables on which they were nurtured, is now no longer given as a gift; today it must be won by man's own efforts. To reach this realm he must first enter the world of pictures, replenishing his stagnant emptiness of soul with flowing movement and colour. For a picture or an imagination works in a living way, affecting not only man's thought-life but penetrating his whole being.

How much more livingly, for example, does T.S. Eliot's picture of *The Hollow Men* work in us than would a dissertation written by Mr. Eliot on the plight of modern man!

So when we read that to attain the second degree of Rosicrucian initiation was to become able to transform ideas into pictures, we can understand that this was a

training designed to lead the student towards the reality of
the hidden world of the spirit.

If we think about Shakespeare's plays and poems from
this point of view, we see how he came to live, as he
unfolded his full powers,. in a swiftly moving world of
pictures. He achieved Aristotle's greatest thing by far –
he became a master of metaphor.

At first, as Lamb has remarked, the dramatist has a hard
time with the poet,who,in both play and narrative poem,
holds up the action in sheer intoxication with language.At
first, too, that language is high-flown and affected, for the
"taffeta phrases, silken terms precise" of Lyly's *Euphues*
were still the fashion.

Thus, in *Two Gentlemen of Verona* (1593), Valentine
angers his friend Proteus by promising him that the latter's beloved, Julia, shall become train-bearer to his own
love, Silvia:

> *She shall be dignified with this high honour :-*
> *To bear my lady's train, lest the base earth*
> *Should from her vesture chance to steal a kiss,*
> *And, of so great a favour growing proud,*
> *Disdain to root the summer-swelling flower*
> *And make rough winter everlastingly.*
>
> *(Two Gentlemen of Verona, II, iv)*

The conceit, charming, artificial and ornate, has no
relation to nature. Yet in the same year, when, in Venus
and Adonis, Venus sees Adonis slain by the boar, there
shines out a little jewel of loving observation which is like
a foreshadowing of the later suffering of his own sensitive
soul:

As the snail, whose tender horns being hit,
Shrinks backwards in his shelly cave with pain,
And there, all smothered up in the shade doth sit
Long after, fearing to creep forth again,
So, at the bloody view, her eyes are fled
Into the deep, dark caverns of her head.

(Venus and Adonis, 1033-39)

Often, as here, the metaphors in this early stage are blossoms of light flashing up from a soil in which, belonging as they do to a quite different element, they have no root. But in his maturer work, Shakespeare develops an incomparable skill in weaving them into a web which supports the onward movement of the inner tragedy, as when the sleep-forsaken Macbeth cries in despair:

Methought I heard a voice cry, "Sleep no more;
Macbeth doth murder sleep" – the innocent sleep,
Sleep that knits up the ravell'd sleeve of care,
The death of each day's life, sore labour's bath,
Balm of hurt minds, great nature's second course,
Chief nourisher on life's feast.

(Macbeth, II, ii)

Or as when Macbeth, having murdered Duncan, reflects:

This Duncan
Hath borne his faculties so meek, hath been
So clear in his great office, that his virtues
Will plead like angels trumpet-tongued against
The deep damnation of his taking-off;
And pity, like a naked, new-born babe

Striding the blast, or heaven's Cherubim horsed
Upon the sightless couriers of the air,
Shall blow the horrid deed in every eye,
That tears shall drown the wind.

(Macbeth, I, vii)

The banished cosmos will keep breaking through, as here, or as in Pericles' shattered

O you powers!
That give heaven countless eyes to view men's acts;
(Pericles, I, i)

Or when Bedford mourns the death of his brother, Henry V:

Hung be the heavens with black, yield day to night!
Comets, importing change of times and states,
Brandish your crystal tresses in the sky,
And with them scourge the bad revolting stars
That have consented unto Henry's death!

(King Henry VI, Part I, I, i)

Even, indeed, in the intellect-bound Hamlet's cry that Laertes' grief over Ophelia's death

Conjures the wandering stars, and makes them stand
Like wonder-wounded hearers.

(Hamlet, V, i)

Sometimes a magical picture emerges from multitudinous calm, clear, careful strokes, as in Enobarbus' pellucid description of Cleopatra's barge:

> *The barge she sat in, like a burnish'd throne,*
> *Burn'd on the water; the poop was beaten gold,*
> *Purple the sails, and so perfumèd that*
> *The winds were love-sick with them; the oars were silver,*
> *Which to the tune of flutes kept stroke, and made*
> *The water which they beat to follow faster,*
> *As amorous of their strokes.*
>
> *(Antony and Cleopatra,* II, ii*)*

Yet one boldly splashed evocative phrase can unleash a raging storm at sea:

> *Thou God of this great vast, rebuke these surges*
> *Which wash both heaven and hell!*
>
> *(Pericles,* III, i*)*

And when Othello is about to kill Desdemona, no virtuosity could have moved the heart so painfully as does his stark and simple cry:

> *Out out the light; and then – put out the light.*
>
> *(Othello,* V, ii*)*

Or that of Iras before Cleopatra's death:

> *The bright day is done,*
> *And we are for the dark.*
>
> *(Antony and Cleopatra,* V, ii*)*

A single word can hold a rounded picture, as when the English rebels are warned to

Unthread *the rude eye of rebellion*
                              (King John, V, iv*)*

Or as when Agrippa characterises the dead Antony:

                    A rarer spirit
Ne'er did steer *humanity.*
                              (Antony and Cleopatra, V, i*)*

A candle can become transparent for the light of life, as when Macbeth hears of the Queen's death:

All our yesterdays have lighted fools
The way to dusty death. Out, out, brief candle!
                              (Macbeth, V, v*)*

Sometimes the picture holds an unwitting premonition of what is to come, as when Lear announces:

                    'Tis our fast intent
To shake all care and business from our age,
Conferring them on younger strengths, while we
Unburden'd crawl *towards death.*
                              (King Lear, I, i*)*

Or as when Sebastian's choice of picture points to an

approaching Phoenix-birth of Prospero's island:

> *Now I will believe*
> *That there are unicorns; that in Arabia*
> *There is one tree, the phoenix throne; one phoenix*
> *At this hour reigning there.*
>
> *(The Tempest, III, iii)*

But there is nothing unwitting about Prospero's apocalyptic prophecy:

> *The cloud-capp'd towers, the gorgeous palaces,*
> *The solemn temples, the great globe itself,*
> *Yea, all it shall inherit, shall dissolve*
> *And, like an unsubstantial pageant faded,*
> *Leave not a wrack behind.*
>
> *(The Tempest, IV, i)*

For Shakespeare's world of pictures has here brought him into the world of spiritual reality behind the world of outer appearances. In the following chapters we will attempt to live over into some of the plays in whose unfolding we can trace the path that led him there.

PART TWO

THE SOUL'S HISTORY:
THE PLAYS

CHAPTER VI

LOVE'S LABOUR'S LOST

> "The ancients considered things divine as
> the only realities, and that all others were
> only the images and shadows of truth".
>   TAYLOR[14]

LOVE'S LABOUR'S LOST is one of Shake-speare's early plays, probably first per-formed in 1593, with Southampton and his circle most in mind; then, after revision and a deepening of its content, given in 1597 before Elizabeth and her Court. It is, in fact, a court play, bubbling with wit and mirth, scintillating with brilliant badinage, verbal fireworks and rapid rapier give-and-take of subtle and ingenious sallies.

The young King of Navarre persuades three of his equally young nobles to join him in a vow to devote three years to philosophic study and an ascetic life – one meal a day; three hours' sleep only; no contact with women. One of these nobles, Berowne, is sceptical of the plan, and reminds the King that in any case the Princess of France is due to arrive in two days' time on an embassy from her father.

The King has the Princess lodged without ceremony in his park; but on going to receive her, he and his three nobles fall in light and light-hearted love with her and her three ladies. Catching each other "sighing and sonneting," they decide to break their vow of ascetic study and instead to indulge in amorous dalliance –

LONGAVILLE: *Shall we resolve to woo these girls of France?*

KING: *And win them, too.*

BEROWNE: *Advance your standards, and upon them, lords!*
Pell-mell, down with them!

(IV, iii)

They come to their wooing disguised as Russians. But the "girls of France", forwarned, are masked and have exchanged with each other the jewels their would-be lovers have sent them, so that each woos the wrong lady. When the wooers retire and then return as themselves, they are mocked mercilessly –

ROSALINE: *Help! Hold his brows! He'll swound.*
                              Why look you pale?

PRINCESS: *What did the Russian whisper in your ear?*

ROSALINE: *That he would wed me, or else die my lover.*

KING: *By my life, my troth,*
I never swore this lady such an oath.
My faith and this the Princess I did give;
I knew her by the jewel on her sleeve.

BEROWNE: *I see the trick on't: here was a consent.*
The ladies did change favours; and then we,
Following the signs, wooed but the sign
of she.
Now, to our perjury to add more terror,
We are again foresworn, in will and error.
(V, ii)

Upon a scene of great merriment enters a sable-clad messenger, announcing the death of the King of France. The Princess, preparing for instant departure, bids Navarre, if he be serious in his love,

Go with speed
To some forlorn and naked hermitage,
Remote from all the pleasures of the world.
If this austere, insociable life
Change not your offer made in heat of blood,
Nip not the gaudy blossoms of your love,
Come at the expiration of the year,
And, by this virgin palm now kissing thine,
I will be thine.
(V, ii)

And to Berowne Rosaline holds up a mirror showing him

A man replete with mocks,
Full of comparisons and wounding flouts,
Which you on all estates will execute
That lie within the mercy of your wit.
To weed this wormwood from your fruitful brain,
And therewithal to win me, if you please.

You shall this twelvemonth term, from day to day,
Visit the speechless sick; your task shall be
With all the fierce endeavour of your wit
To enforce the painèd impotent to smile.
BEROWNE: *A twelvemonth! Well, befall what will befall,*
           I'll jest a twelvemonth on a hospital …
           Our wooing doth not end like an old play;
           Jack hath not Jill …

                              (V,ivi)

Goethe records[15] that, while a young student at Strasbourg University, he made a special study of this play.
This was during a period when his spiritual perceptions
received a sudden deepening. One had therefore little
doubt that Goethe was among those who took Shakespeare's points in this play readily enough, especially in
view of the fact that "Shakespeare accompanied Goethe
as an educator and guide throughout his life."[16]

What were these points?

In *Sonnet LXVII*, Shakespeare asks:

   Why should poor beauty indirectly seek
   Roses of shadow, since his rose is true?

Love's Labour's Lost, on the surface a *tour-de-force* of
coruscating frivolity, has at another level a validity as
the soul's history of youth, indirectly seeking one rose of
shadow after another on a life-journey whose proper
consummation, whose flowering of the spirit, is the
finding of the true rose.

---

[15] DICHTUNG UND WAHRHEIT, BK XI

[16] Rudolf Steiner: DRAMA IN RELATION TO EDUCATION (Lecture
   given at Stratford-on-Avon on April 10th, 1922)

The King of Navarre's proposition of three years'
ascetic study is a rose of shadow. Its *raison d'etre* is a
wrong one (in *The Chymical Wedding* the true seekers after
knowledge are silent and humble and avoid all show) –

> KING: *Let fame, that all hunt after in their lives,*
> *Live registered upon our brazen tombs,*
> *And make us heirs of all eternity.*
> (I, i)

It would divorce learning from reality, dealing only in
"names" and the cataloguing of facts, since it exiles the
heart, and only the heart gives access to true wisdom–

> BEROWNE: *Study is like the heaven's glorious sun,*
> *That will not be deep-searched with saucy*
>   *looks.*
> *Small have continual plodders ever won,*
> *Save base authority from others' books.*
> *These earthly godfathers of heaven's lights*
> *That give a name to every fixèd star*
> *Have no more profit of their shining nights*
> *Than those that walk and wot not what they*
>   *are.*
> *Too much to know is to know nought but fame;*
> *And every godfather can give a name.*
> (I, i)

(Though the King hits neatly back at this with his riposte:

How well he's read, to reason against reading!)

It is chasing a chimera:

> BEROWNE: *So, ere you find where light in darkness lies,*
> *Your light grows dark by losing of your eyes.*
>   *(I, i)*

Above all, such premature withdrawal from the outer world and its experiences sidesteps the duties and responsibilities of life:

> BEROWNE: *So study evermore is overshot.*
> *While it would study to have what it would,*
> *It doth forget to do the thing it should.*
>   *(I, i)*

What, for example about the immanent embassy of the Princess of France? At which reminder the King confesses naïvely:

> *Why, this was quite forgot!*

When the King and his three lords visit the Princess and her three ladies and fall lightly in love, it is a fancy engendered in the eyes; it is another rose of shadow. Berowne indites to Rosaline a sonnet full of high-flown sentiments:

> *If knowledge be the mark, to know thee shall suffice.*
> *All ignorant that soul that sees thee without wonder ...*

Celestial as thou art, O pardon, love, this wrong,
That sing's heaven's praises with such an earthly tongue.

(IV, ii)

It is indeed an earthly tongue in his gross jests and
soliloquies concerning her. It is also a tongue-in-the-
cheek; the conventions of light love-making demand
hypocritical hyperbole. He does not really think of her
in terms of *celestial* and *heaven*; he thinks of her in terms
of earthly senses and of earthly sensuality. Yet, many
a true word being spoken in jest, he is voicing his future
fate, for his finding of the true rose will, via this rose of
shadow, this mere philandering, include his finding of
"the Venus of the sky", of Aphrodite Urania.

And now Berowne is twice a hypocrite, for hearing the
other three reading aloud *their* sonnets, he crows with
self-righteous indignation:

Now step I forth to whip hypocrisy.
Are you not ashamed? Nay, are you not,
All three of you, to be thus much o'ershot?
I am betrayed by keeping company
With men like you. When shall you hear that I
Will praise a hand, a foot, a face, an eye,
A gait, a state, a brow, a breast, a waist,
A leg, a limb?

(IV, iii)

In point of fact they hear immediately, his sonnet being
put into the King's hand by mistake; and when he has
confessed –

He, he and you, and you my liege, and I
Are pick-purses in love –

he is begged by the King to "prove our loving lawful",
and by Demaine to produce "some salve for perjury".
In his reply –

Let us lose our oaths to find ourselves,
Or else we lose ourselves to keep our oaths –

that finding of oneself which is to become one of the
central themes of Shakespeare's plays is spotlit for the
first time. Self-knowledge is revealed as an aspect of the
true rose youth is seeking,
But to the finding of the true rose in others all four young
men have still to be awakened. Masked and disguised as
Russians, they visit the ladies, who are, however, aware
of their identities, so that the Princess is justified in her
remark:

We are wise girls to mock our lovers so.
                                              (V, ii)

For it is by means of merriment that Shakespeare,
throughout this play, reveals and dismisses as not being
the object of the quest each rose of shadow as it comes
along; it is the ladies' laughter that makes the four young
men aware that they have been misled by the masks and
exchanged jewels – by mere externals; they have still to
pierce the visor of the face, the garment of the body, to
reach the essential being of the soul. Growth in finding

one's own self is to go hand-in-hand with growth of
recognition of the "I" in other.
Berowne, already the most advanced in self-knowledge,
is the first to seize the point –

> *The ladies did change favours; and then we,*
> *Following the signs, wooed but the sign of she.*

So "we are again foresworn" – this time by making our
vows to the wrong lady. He thinks of it in the sense of
mistaking one lady for another; the ladies (and Shakespeare) think of it in the sense of mistaking the bodily
beauty of each lady for her true self – that, too, is wooing
but the sign of she. Rosaline has already intimated this
when the King, believing her to be the Princess, begs her
to unmask:

> KING: *Vouchsafe, bright moon, and these thy stars*
> *to shine,*
> *Those clouds removed, upon our watery eyne.*
> ROSALINE: *O vain petitioner! Beg a greater matter.*
> *Thou now request'st but moonshine in the water.*
> *(V, ii)*

This "greater matter" – the recognition of the true rose
incarnated in each lady, of the immortal being within
her mortal garment – is a revelation too solemn to be
carried by the thistledown mood of the play. Some death-
experience is necessary before great revelations can come
to pass; "he who knows not dying and becoming", says
Goethe, "is but a guest lost on this dark earth"; and that

death is Sebastian's phoenix-throne is the theme of *The Chymical Wedding*. In later plays the death-experience cuts nearer and nearer to the bone, as with Cordelia's death in *King Lear*; in a play of such levity as *Love's Labour's Lost*, it can be neither so immediate nor so shattering. In the news of the death of the distant King of France it comes, as it were, twice removed.

Now there appear for the first time those tests preceding marriage which Shakespeare lays on lovers again and again, right up to Ferdinand's log-hauling in *The Tempest*. The King is ripe now for a year of "the life removed"; love will warm learning. Berowne is given the same space of time to turn his wormwood wit into the healing medicine of compassion.

Will they pass their tests?

The play does not say. But the King says:

> *For ever then my heart is in thy breast.*

and Berowne:

> *Behold the window of my heart, mine eye,*
> *What humble suit attends thy answer there.*
> (V, ii)

These two remarks could well be among those points with a significance for the judicious, for both carry an echo of *Sonnet XLVI*:

> *Mine eye's due is thine outward part,*
> *And my heart's right thine inward love of heart.*

Shakespeare is here using the gay science (*le gai savoir*),
that Templar language which became the secret
language of the troubadours. Dante, who also wrote in it,
gives a hint as to its understanding when he says, "By
heart I mean the inward secret", and Rossetti tells us:
"In the secret language called the Gay Science, *heart*
meant the hidden secret, *face* the outward meaning,
sighs the verses written in this vocabulary." [17] What the
King then seems to be saying is that his hidden secret,
his true rose, is in the keeping of the true rose of the
Princess; and Berowne that his outer being has become
transparent for his inner self, and both are Rosaline's.

So, in *Love's Labour's Lost*, we stand beside the cradle of
Shakespeare's new-born task – to guide man down into
egohood and back to apprehension of the Spirit behind
matter.We watch his first prentice preoccupation with
a mermaid theme which he was to continue to unfold
further in pay after play, culminating in it glorious climax
in *The Tempest* – the theme of Plato's World of Ideas.
Renaissance Rosicrucianism spoke much of this – of a
spiritual world which stands behind the physical one,
veiled to modern eyes by matter, yet which is its very
fount and origin, so that all that seems to us so actual in
the sense-world is, as it were, an image of that invisible
order which in ancient times was still visible and which
then was considered the true reality. During the period
since, as Bacon said, he "sounded a trumpet for the new
science", with its consequent loss of this inner vision, it
has been a Rosicrucian task to hold open, for use in the
future, the door between two worlds – of sensible
phenomena and of supersensible archetypes, of roses of
shadow and of the true rose; and it was part of Shakespeare's task to blaze the way back to that door.

[17] HISTORY OF THE ANTIPAPAL SPIRIT THAT PRECEDED THE REFORMATION

In 1593, when *Love's Labour's Lost*, was first performed, Shakespeare was twenty-nine years old, and it was only eight years since he had come to London. Even allowing for a phenomenally swift hatching of gifted dramatist out of country cousin, the worlds opened up to him at the Mermaid must still in 1593 have been spectacularly brave new worlds to him. If one asks which one he would feel most urgently upon his pulses, one's immediate answer is: Plato's World of Ideas. For every true artist, whatever his medium, whenever he "gets an idea" for his work, gets it from there. In clothing it he obscures it, and all his artistic strivings are towards one end – that this clothing may achieve an ever clearer transparency, through which his rose of shadow may as purely and precisely as his powers permit portray the true rose behind it.

We can see then that it was inevitable that a process Shakespeare could watch taking place in the realm of his own creative activity should itself become a rose he would early strive to bring to earth.

Since the medium of Shakespeare's art was speech, one can also understand why, among all the gods and goddesses and myths and Mysteries to be met with at the Mermaid, it was to Diana, the pre-Christian guardian of the Creative Word, and to her Mysteries of Ephesus, that he was specially drawn. Already in *The Comedy of Errors*, written in the same year as *Love's Labour's Lost*, the scene is laid at Ephesus; in *Pericles*, much later, Diana and her Temple at Ephesus are to play a fundamental part. So, in *A Midsummer Night's Dream*, does Dian's bud. In the new qualities which Marina, Perdita and Miranda bring to the new race, they are all three "Diana's nuns".

It was at Ephesus that the early Greek philosophers proclaimed the secrets of the Logos. "In the Temple the
Initiates were taught to experience what afterwards
found such perfect expression in the Gospel of St. John –
'In the beginning was the Word. And the Word was
with God. And the Word was God.'[18] The pupils were
led before the statue of Diana. Identifying himself with
this statue which was fulness of life, which abounded
everywhere with life, the pupil lived his way into the
cosmic ether. The real nature of human speech was
revealed to him; and then, from this human image of the
Cosmic Logos, it was shown how the Cosmic Word
works and weaves creatively throughout the universe."[19]
The most ancient statues of Diana were of ebony. She
was black because she represented those hidden fountains
of life out of which all things created came forth. She has
Christian counterparts in the Black Madonnas who were
once so deeply reverenced in different parts of Europe,
and who can still be seen today, for instance, at Chartres
and Monserrat.

In *Love's Labour's Lost* so much emphasis is laid upon the
blackness of Rosaline that it seems it must surely point to
something beyond herself, something even beyond the
Dark Lady of the Sonnets, and that here must have been
one of Shakespeare's hidden clues for the judicious.
While the otherwise featureless Katherine's "hairs" are
amber, the sparkling Rosaline has

> *Two pitch balls stuck in her face for eyes,*
> *(III, i)*

and the banter to which Berowne is subjected when his
three companions find his sonnet to her consists entirely

---

[18] GOSPEL ACCORDING TO ST. JOHN, I, i
[19] Rudolf Steiner: WORLD HISTORY

of variations of the same theme:

KING: *By heaven, thy love is black as ebony!*
BEROWNE: *Is ebony like her? O wood divine!*
                     A wife of such wood were felicity...
                     No face is fair that is not full so black...
                     O! if in black my lady's brows be deck'd,
                     Then therefore is she born to make black fair.
DUMAINE: *To look like her are chimney-sweepers black.*
LONGAVILLE: *And since her time are colliers counted*
                                                                   bright.
KING: *And Ethiops of their sweet complexion*
                                                                   crack.
DUMAINE: *Dark needs no candles now, for dark is*
                                                                   light.
                              (IV, iii)

The indications seems to be that Rosaline's true rose is to
be found in Diana's kingdom of creative forces, which is
also Plato's World of Ideas and Goethe's Realm of the
Mothers. And in case any among the judicious have
failed to take the point, Shakespeare proceeds to make it
more explicit by equating Rosaline with the moon:

ROSALINE: *My face is but a moon, and clouded too.*
KING: *Vouchsafe, bright moon, and these thy stars,*
                   to shine.
ROSALINE: *Thou now request'st but moonshine in the*
                   water ...
                   You took the moon at full, but now she's chang'd.
KING: *Yet still she is the moon, and I the man.*
                              (V, iii)

To Dante, Beatrice was both herself and his leader in the soul-world. In *Love's Labour's Lost* Rosaline stands like Berowne's guide into the realm of the Creative Word. She seeks to "weed this wormwood" from a tongue "replete with mocks". And to her and because of her, Berowne pledges himself to a larger sincerity and simplicity of speech.

> *Taffeta phrases, silken terms precise,*
> *Three-pil'd hyperboles, spruce affection,*
> *Figures pedantical: these summer flies*
> *Have blown me full of maggot ostentation,*
> *I do foreswear them; and I here protest,*
> *By this white glove,– how white the hand, God knows –*
> *Henceforth my wooing mind shall be express'd*
> *In russet yeas and honest kersey noes.*
>
> *(V, ii)*

One suspects that, throughout, Berowne may well have been speaking with the voice of Shakespeare. Certainly Berowne's pledge was a prelude to Shakespeare's own growth into language of such limpidity that, only two years later, *A Midsummer Night's Dream* contained some of the loveliest lyric poetry he was ever to write. We shall consider in the next chapter its further soul-excursions into Plato's World of Ideas, and its first tentative intimations of other aspects of Shakespeare's task.

CHAPTER VII

A MIDSUMMER NIGHT'S DREAM

"I have surely a piece of Divinity in me;
something that was before the elements".
SIR THOMAS BROWNE[20]

A MIDSUMMER NIGHT'S DREAM has been called Shakespeare's "first incomparable and immortal masterpiece". It might almost be described as a dramatic lyric. The poetry is exquisite; the dramatic tension at no time rises to a great height. Its creator has his mind on other matters.

The play was given at a wedding of a noble couple of the Court in 1595. Since this would automatically be attended by "divers of worship" of the Mermaid circle, the occasion provided Shakespeare with an audience ready and able to take his finer "points".

It has been said of the "Wood near Athens" in which most of the action takes place that it is a good deal nearer to Stratford than to Athens. Certainly its Duke's oak at which the "rude mechanicals" meet to rehearse their play, its hawthorn-brake which Quince offers them as a

[20] RELIGIO MEDICI

tiring-room, its bank of wild thyme on which Titania sleeps, its faint primrose-beds, its cowslips tall, its nodding violets, its sweet musk-roses, its luscious woodbine, Bottom's finch, sparrow, lark and plainsong cuckoo, Puck's russet-pated choughs – certainly all these are sights and sounds from the Forest of Arden stored up in his memory by a restless and lawless youth with the sensitive mind of a poet.

Yet the Wood near Athens is not really an earthly wood at all. It is the first of Shakespeare's extra-mundane regions – others are Belmont in *The Merchant of Venice*, the Coast of Bohemia in *The Winter's Tale*, the Sea off Mitylene in *Pericles*, Prospero's Island in *The Tempest* – all belonging to an unlikely, magical topography, all bathed in a light that never was on sea or land.

The Wood near Athens is, in fact, a wood out of a fairytale. In the fairytale wood only those who know it well (such as the Woodsman) or those who drop peas from their pockets to mark the way (such as Hansel) do not go astray. For it is a picture of a super-abundance of those invisible forces which we have already seen as working and weaving within and behind the physical world. And that craves wary walking.

Two extra factors make that wood, that night, crave doubly wary walking. One is that (despite the play's title), Theseus' remark when he finds the four lovers asleep in the wood –

> *No doubt they rose up early to observe*
> *The rite of May –*
>
> (IV, i)

makes it clear that the wanderings in the wood took place

on May Eve, Walpurgis Night, when those superabund-
ant forces are already disturbed.

The second is that, as Titania indicates, this sphere of
elemental ether has been further disturbed by the quarrel
between herself and Oberon, bringing about the chaotic
weather of 1594:

> *The seasons alter; hoary-headed frosts*
> *Fall in the fresh lap of the crimson rose…*
> *And this same progeny of evil comes*
> *From our debate, from our dissension;*
> *We are their parents and original.*
>
> *(II, i)*

For both Titania and Oberon are elemental Nature
Spirits (and, as they each remind us, "of no common
sort"), and are therefore closely interwoven with this
world of borderland forces.

And now into this disorder is introduced Cupid's flower.
This is how Oberon describes its genesis:

> *I sat upon a promontory,*
> *And heard a mermaid on a dolphin's back*
> *Uttering such dulcet and harmonious breath*
> *That the rude sea grew civil at her song,*
> *And certain stars shot madly from their spheres*
> *To hear the sea-maid's music.*
> *That very time I saw,*
> *Flying between the cold moon and the earth,*
> *Cupid all arm'd: a certain aim he took*
> *At a fair vestal thronèd by the west,*
> *And loos'd his love-shaft smartly from his bow,*

As it should pierce a hundred thousand hearts;
But I might see young Cupid's fiery shaft
Quench'd in the chaste beams of the watery moon,
And the imperial votaress passed on,
In maiden-meditation, fancy-free.
Yet mark'd I where the bolt of Cupid fell:
It fell upon a little western flower,
Before milk-white, now purple with love's wound,
And maidens call it Love-in-idleness.
                              (II, i)

So the song of the sirens – by which, Christian Rosenkreutz tells us in *The Chymical Wedding*, he himself was
moved "in a way which tended little to my credit," and
by which, as Oberon tells us here, even the harmony of
the heavens can be disturbed – unites with Cupid's love-
shaft to wound the milk-white flower. In Shakespeare's
time, *idleness* could mean *intoxication, delirium*; and it is
indeed a kind of delirium that the juice of love-in-idleness
induces in both Demetrius and Lysander. Its wound has
invaded a realm which is rightfully Diana's. Yet it is
potent magic; and like other forms of delirium, even
delirium tremens, it can open the eyes it touches to sight in
other dimensions.

In *Love's Labour's Lost*, Shakespeare had united in one
being each true rose and its shadow, each archetype and
its embodiment; Rosaline for example, embraced both.
In *A Midsummer Night's Dream* he depicts them apart.
One can often find the key to a Shakespeare character in
his name – Perdita is the lost one; Miranda the wondrous
one; Marina is born at sea; Parolles is a liar; Lafeu
exposes him; Posthumous is, in the Mystery sense, born
after death; in Fidele, Imogen is maligned but faithful.

In Hermia's name one has an echo both of Hermetic, hidden, and of Hermes, the heavenly messenger, the link between the worlds of gods and men. So already her name points to her as one coming direct from the realm of Ideas, while Helena recalls Helen, the prototype of *earthly* beauty.

Helena longs to model herself faithfully on Hermia –

> *Your tongue's sweet air*
> *More tuneable than lark to shepherd's ear*
> *When wheat is green, when hawthorn buds appear.*
> *Sickness is catching: O! were favour so,*
> *Yours would I catch, fair Hermia, ere I go.*
> *My ear should catch your voice, my eye your eye;*
> *My tongue should catch your tongue's sweet melody.*
> *Were the world mine, Demetrius being bated,*
> *The rest I'd give to be to you translated.*
>
> *(I, i)*

Later, grieving over what seems to her to be Hermia's mockery when the love-juice has set them at cross-purposes, Helena appeals to their inseparability:

> *In all the counsels that we two have shar'd,*
> *The sister-vows, the hours that we have spent,*
> *When we have chid the hasty-footed time*
> *For parting us, O! is it all forgot?*
> *All school-days' friendship, childhood innocence?*
> *We, Hermia, like two artificial* gods,*
> *Have with our neelds created both one flower,*
> *Both on one sampler, sitting on one cushion,*
> *Both warbling of one song, both in one key,*

* skilful

As if our hands, our sides, voices, and minds,
Had been incorporate. So we grew together,
Like to a double cherry, seeming parted,
But yet an union in partition;
Two lovely berries moulded on one stem;
So, with two seeming bodies, but one heart;
Two of the first, like coats in heraldry,
Due but to one, and crownèd with one crest.
And will you rend our ancient love asunder?
                                    (III, ii)

And later yet, when the gloves are off, their difference in substantiality is contrasted. Hermia is characterised as little, low, you puppet you, you dwarf, you minimus, you bead, you acorn! Helena is thou painted maypole, and with her personage, her tall personage, her height forsooth! Helena sums up:

Your hands than mine are quicker for a fray;
My legs are longer, though, to run away.
                                    (III, ii)

Hermia, again, is dark, as Rosaline was dark. When the love-juice in his eyes has deflected Lysander's love from her to Helena, he cruelly drives her from him with:

Away, you Ethiop...!
Out, tawny Tartar, out!
                                    (III, ii)

And to Helena he protests:

> *Not Hermia, but Helena I love:*
> *Who will not change a raven for a dove?*
>
> *(II, ii)*

While Helena's pale loveliness is emphasised when Demetrius wakes with *his* love changed by the love-juice in *his* eyes:

> *O! Helen, goddess, nymph, perfect, divine!*
> *O! let me kiss*
> *This princess of pure white!*
>
> *(III, ii)*

Helena, making Hermia's hidden beauty apparent in the sense-world, is marked out to be the true mate for Demetrius, whose very name, speech-related to that of Demeter, the Earth-Goddess, points to his connection with life on earth. So his first love – his love for Helena – was his right and predestined love; and when his heart strays to Hermia, Oberon enchants it back to its true abiding-place:

> *Flower of this purple dye,*
> *Hit with Cupid's archery,*
> *Sink in apple of his eye.*
> *When his love he doth espy,*
> *Let her shine as gloriously*
> *As the Venus of the sky.*
>
> *(II, ii)*

That is, let Helena, his earthly love, then shine glori-
ously for him as Hermia, his heavenly love, does now.
When Lysander, equally Hermia's true, predestined
lover, wakes enamoured of Helena, it is not really Helena
but the Hermia-Idea in Helena that he now loves; his
first words, spoken in the gay science, reveal the secret:

> *Transparent Helena! Natures shows art,*
> *That through thy bosom makes me see thy heart.*
> *(II, ii)*

To lead him back to Hermia herself, Oberon resorts to
the magic of that divine being whose rightful realm this
is, giving Dian's bud to Puck with the injunction:

> *Crush this herb into Lysander's eye:*
> *Whose liquor hath this virtuous property,*
> *To take from thence all error with his might,*
> *And make his eyeballs roll with wonted sight.*
> *When they next wake, all this derision*
> *Shall seem a dream and fruitless vision;*
> *And back to Athens shall the lovers wend,*
> *With league whose date till death shall never end.*
> *(III, ii)*

Meanwhile, Oberon, to punish Titania for withholding
her Indian boy from him, charms her eyes with Cupid's
flower, while Puck bewitches Bottom, fixing "an ass's
nowl" upon his head. For Titania, also, love-in-idleness
works like soma or mescalin or the sacred mushroom –
draws back a veil; and as, by the short-cut of a vegetable
magic, Lysander had seen the Hermia within Helena, so
Titania sees the angel within the rude mechanical.

What angel wakes me from my flowery bed?...
I pray thee, gentle mortal, sing again:
My ear is much enamour'd of thy note;
So is mine eye enthrallèd to thy shape;
And thy fair virtue's force, perforce, doth move me,
On the first view, to say, to swear, I love thee ...
Thou art as wise as thou art beautiful...
Pease-blossom! Cobweb! Moth! and Mustard-seed!
Be kind and courteous to this gentlemen

(III, i)

And Bottom is indeed a gentleman. He greets his fairy
henchmen with great courtesy –

I cry your worship's mercy, heartily ... I pray you,
commend me to your mother and your father,
good Master Cobweb ...
I shall desire you of more acquaintance, good Master
Mustard-Seed ...

(III, i)

And, when he does ask a service of them, he does so with
the greatest consideration –

Do not fret yourself too much in the action, mounsieur.

(IV, i)

There is modesty and even a certain delicacy in his
passive response to Titania's wooing, and a robust dis-
cretion when, in reply to her

Come, sit thee down upon this flowery bed.,
While I thy amiable cheeks do coy,
And stick musk-roses on thy sleek smooth head,
And kiss thy fair large ears, my gentle joy,
                              (IV, i)

he asks for 'Cavalery Cobweb to scratch "his "marvellous hairy" face.
Puck shows elvish acumen in the form his bewitchment
of Bottom takes, for it is with that beast of burden, the
Brother Ass of his body, that Bottom serves the community; Philostrate describes him and his fellows to
Theseus as

Hard-handed men, that work in Athens here,
Which never labour'd in their minds till now,
And now have toil'd their unbreath'd memories
With this same play, against your nuptial.
                              (V, i)

(And if Midas' preference for Pan's pipes rather than
Apollo's lyre won him ass's ears, it is not surprising –
however disconcerting – if Bottoms partiality for the
tongs and the bones should do the same.)
But Puck looks no deeper than the rose's shadow when
he dismisses Bottom as

The shallowest thick-skin of that barren sort.
                              (III, i)

For it is Bottom without whom the wedding-play will
collapse, who is master of all situations, who has such

wide sympathies that he can live over into all the play's
parts at once, who is concerned not to scare the ladies,
who reminds his fellows to have good strings to their
beards, who would utter sweet breath. Even when he is
dead he will not lie down, but pops up again to end
Pyramus and Thisbe as *Romeo and Juliet* ends –

No, I assure you;
The wall is down that parted their fathers.
(V, i)

When Oberon releases Titania's "charmèd eye"–

Be as thou wast wont to be;
See as thou wast wont to see;
Dian's bud o'er Cupid's flower
Hath such force and blessed power –
(IV, i)

the piece of Divinity in Bottom is obscured, disguised
again for her by the hempen homespun of his body –

O! how mine eye do loathe his visage now.
(IV, i)

And Bottom, awaking alone, meanders in his mind:

I have had a most rare vision. I have had a dream,
past the wit of man to say what dream it was;
man is but an ass if he go about to expound this

dream, methought I was – there is no man can
tell what. Methought I was, – and methought I
had, – but man is but a patched fool if he will
offer to say what methought I had. The eye of man hath
not heard, the ear of man hath not seen, man's hand
is not able to taste, his tongue to conceive, nor his
heart to report, what my dream was.
                                                    (IV, i)

We take it for granted that he is being afflicted by visitations of his "transformed scalp". But need that necessarily be all? Hermia, reviewing that night's workings of Cupid's flower, remarks:

Methinks I see these things with parted eye,
When everything seems double.
                                                    (IV, i)

may not Bottom also be seeing these same things with parted eye – on the one hand being marvellous hairy about the face and desiring a peck of provender; on the other, in an instant of borrowed clairvoyance, seeing a most rare vision of his essential self such as Donne was later to see? –
"In a flash, at a trumpet crash, this Jack, joke, poor potsherd, patch, matchwood, immortal diamond is – immortal diamond."

In *A Midsummer Night's Dream* Shakespeares introduces a second theme connected with mankind's development which is to occupy him in succeeding plays, coming to a painful climax in *King Lear* – the dawn of free will versus the blood-tie. Demetrius at the opening of the play has transferred his love from Helena to Hermia, whose father has given him permission to marry her. If Hermia does not obey, she must either die or become one of "Diana's nuns".

> *To live a barren sister all your life,*
> *Chanting faint hymns to the cold fruitless moon.*
>   *(I, i)*

But Hermia and Lysander love each other, and even Theseus' ducal injunction to fit her fancies to her father's will cannot break her own –

> *O hell! To choose love by another's eye.*
>   *(I, i)*

One can imagine how, when Theseus embarked on his urbane persuasion–

> *To you, your father should be as a god;*
> *One that compos'd your beauties, yea, and one*
> *To whom you are but as a form in wax*
> *By him imprinted, and within his power*
> *To leave the figure or disfigure it –*
>   *(I, i)*

the "judicious" in the audience would be alerted, for the words were Plato's, but not the sentiment. What Plato had said was that "the visible world bears the impress of the World of Ideas, imprinted on it like a seal on wax". Your father provided the wax; but it was the signature of our own "I" upon it that was of prime importance. There have been Mr. Barretts of Wimpole Street right down to our own day; but in Shakespeare's the ego just emerging into self-awareness was already beginning its struggle to establish its own self-sovereignty.

Demetrius, his eyes charmed by Cupid's love-juice while he lay sleeping in the wood, re-bestowed his love on Helena, thus opening the way for Hermia's and Lysander's true-love to run smooth. But that such a solution could be found only in a midsummer night's dream as long as fathers were as gods, Shakespeare made clear in his Interlude of Pyramus and Thisbe.

It is always enlightening to examine a play-within-a-play in relation to the play it is within. This was a new device which had appeared only in Shakespeare's day, being first used by Kyd in his *Spanish Tragedy* in 1589, Shakespeare's fourth year in London. Against the background of the age, one can see it as a heightening of the Elizabethans' new experience of sharpened consciousness.

Shakespeare uses it to pinpoint or to highlight some problem or situation central to the play itself. Thus, in *Hamlet* the play within the play is a microscopic copy of the crime out of which the whole play sprang, and is designed to focus that crime before the conscience of the king and so spur Hamlet himself into action. The Masque in *The Tempest* draws back the curtain to reveal Juno and Ceres, the divine prototypes of marriage made in heaven and earthly fruitfulness; it is, as it were, the spiritual blueprint of the betrothal just contracted between Ferdinand and Miranda.

In *A Midsummer Night's Dream* the interlude of Pyramus and Thisbe is a kind of miniature parody, at once "merry and tragical", of the play's confusions and cross-purposes,

the parody given laborious point by Moonshine with his
lantern and his thornbush.

Reading beforehand the players' description of the Interlude ("A tedious brief scene of young Pyramus and his
love Thisbe; very tragical mirth"), Theseus muses:

> *Merry and tragical! Tedious and brief!*
> *That is, hot ice and wondrous strange snow.*
> *How shall we find the concord of this discord?*
>
> *(V, i)*

And, coming upon the four lovers peacefully asleep
together after all their discords, he asks:

> *I know you two are rival enemies;*
> *How comes this gentle concord in the world,*
> *That hatred is so far from jealousy,*
> *To sleep by hate, and fear no enmity?*
>
> *(IV, i)*

The Ancient Mysteries taught that it was by a balance of
polarities – love and hate, peace and strife, attraction and
repulsion – and by the separation of spirit and matter
and their reunion, that the cosmos was kept constant in its
allotted form. It was from the contentious marriage of
Mars and Venus that Harmonia was born. At her marriage to Cadmus she was given a peplos woven by Athene
herself and a wonderful necklace made by Vulcan; in
Phoenicia she was venerated as the balanced order of
material Creation, and about her neck hung the jewels
of the harmonised universe.

Something of this descended to the Greek philosophers

(in particular, Empedocles), and something again to the troubadours. "Before Dante lived, the Gay Science had fixed the foundation of its language on the two words, love and hatred; and all their attendant qualities followed on each side – pleasure and grief, truth and falsehood, light and darkness, sun and moon, life and death, good and evil, virtue and vice. Courage and cowardice, mountain and valley, fire and frost, garden and desert."[21]
One finds these antitheses a favourite theme in the sonnets, as, for example, in *Sonnet XXXV*:

> *Such civil war is in my love and hate,*
> *That I am accessary needs must be*
> *To that sweet thief which sourly robs from me.*

Both strife between contraries and their union often appear in the plays. The plot of *All's Well that Ends Well* revolves round this polarity of love and hate; and in *A Midsummer Night's Dream*, Lysander, with Cupid's love-juice in his eyes, again and again speaks hatefully of hate to his love Hermia:

> *The hate I bear thee made me leave thee so ...*
> *Out, loathed medicine! Hated poison, hence! ...*
> *I do hate thee and love Helena.*
>
> *(III, ii)*

But, out of their night of discord, from their Mars and Venus, a new Harmonia is born. They have found balance; they have mellowed; they have known wonder; they have grown while they slept.

---

[21] Rossetti: HISTORY OF THE ANTIPAPAL SPIRIT THAT PRECEDED THE REFORMATION

DEMETRIUS: *These things seem small and*
                                          indistinguishable,
                          Like far-off mountains turnèd into clouds
HERMIA: *Methinks I see these things with parted eye,*
                  When everything seems double.
HELENA: *So methinks:*
                  And I have found Demetrius, like a jewel,
                  Mine own, and not mine own.
DEMETRIUS: *Are you sure*
                  We are awake? It seems to me
                  That yet we sleep, we dream
                                   (IV, i)

Theseus and Hippolyta stand outside the sphere of the wood of error, remote, of mythical proportions. Today we think of Theseus as a Sun-hero who wrought mighty deeds in the sphere of the human intellect, slaying the minotaur lurking in the labyrinth of man's brain, receiving from Ariadne the precious clue of logical thought to guide man safely through its mazes. Hippolyta we know as a representative of the heart-system in man in the very special way pictured in the Amazons' lopping of the breast which could impede their archery's true aim.

To our amazement (but need we, after all, be so astonished?) Shakespeare portrays them out of a background which takes all this as understood. In Theseus it is the head that comments astringently on the night's madness, and it is Hippolyta's heart that goes out with warmth to understand it –

HIPPOLYTA:
'Tis strange, my Theseus, that these lovers speak of.

THESEUS: *More strange than true. I never may believe*
     These antique fables, nor these fairy toys.
     Lovers and madmen have such seething
               brains,
     Such shaping fantasies, that apprehend
     More than cool reason ever comprehends.
HIPPOLYTA: *But all their minds transfigurèd so together,*
     More witnesseth than fancy's images,
     *And grows to something of great constancy.**
       (V, i)

Yet it is Theseus who gives us probably the most inspired and precise description we have in the English language of how, in creative art, the Idea descends into incarnation, of how the Hermia becomes the Helena:

The poet's eye, in a fine frenzy rolling,
Doth glance from heaven to earth, from earth to heaven;
And as imagination bodies forth
The forms of things unknown, the poet's pen
Turns them to shapes, and gives to airy nothing
A local habitation and a name.
       (V, i)

In not believing "these fairy toys", Theseus was a man of the new age. Such disbelief is so general today that it comes as a shock to realize that in Shakespeare's time fairies were a serious issue between Papists and Puritans. The latter considered them "an invention of Popery" and fought hard to stamp out such "fantastical superstitions" – so hard that Richard Corbet,who was three years old when *A Midsummer Night's Dream* was written, was later

* consistency

himself to write of how fairies had been driven out of England:

> ... *"Witness those rings and roundelays*
> *Of theirs which yet remain*
> *Were rooted in Queen Mary's days*
> *On many a grassy plain.*
> *But since of late Elizabeth*
> *And later James came in,*
> *They never dance on any heath*
> *As when the time had been.*
> *And all your children stol'n from thence*
> *Are grown puritanes ..."* [22]

It was therefore quite an audacious gesture of defiance of the city fathers on the part of Shakespeare to put fairies on the stage, even though most of his audience, gentle and simple, still privately believed whole-heartedly in them. What was left of them by Cromwell's time the latter stamped out with the other traditions and arts rooted on that pictorial consciousness which the national destiny demanded must for a time be sacrificed in the interests of the new scientific and materialist culture. It is therefore a gift to our own time that Shakespeare has made in planting this delicate and radiant picture of the fairy world in our national heritage, for us to carry with us like a tiny talisman through the dark days till, like Goethe, we are able actually to see Ideas again.

"Jack shall have Jill," says Puck in this play, as if in answer to Berowne's "Jack hath not Jill" in *Love's Labour's Lost*. In the latter play the tests were still left unresolved; now in *The Merchant of Venice* we can watch Shakespeare resolving them magnificently.

[22] THE FAIRIES' FAREWELL

CHAPTER VIII

THE MERCHANT OF VENICE

"Art is to be regarded as the capacity of creating a whole that is inspired by an invisible order; and its aim is to guide the human soul".

PLATO [23]

CONTEMPORARY events and an old Italian story come together to provide the raw material of *The Merchant of Venice*. In 1590 an Italian, Antonio Perez, and a Jewish physician, Dr. Lopez had come to England together. In 1594 Lopez was convicted of plotting both to assassinate Antonio and to poison Elizabeth; at and following his trial and execution, public feeling against the Jews rose to fever heat in London.

Taking this tide in full, a rival theatre was soon playing Marlowe's *Jew of Malta* to crowded houses. The Lord Chamberlain's men – Shakespeare's company – in turn demanded of The Globe's playwright a play with the same topical drawing capacity. Shakespeare wrote one.

But in it the hatred which possessed the mob was passed

[23] PHAEDRUS

through his heart's crucible. The public shall have their Jew-baiting; but they shall also be brought face to face with the question: Who made Shylock what he is?

Hath not a Jew eyes? Hath not a Jew hands, organs,
senses, affections, passions? If you prick us, do
we not bleed? If you poison us, do we not die?
And if you wrong us, shall we not revenge? If
a Jew wrong a Christian, what is his humility?
Revenge. If a Christian wrong a Jew, what
shall his sufferance be by Christian example?
Why, revenge. The villainy you teach me I
will execute, and it shall go hard but I will
better the instruction.

(III, i)

And again:

Thou call'st me dog before thou had'st a cause.
But, since I am a dog, beware my fangs.

(III, iii)

In *Sir Thomas More*, a playscript now in the British Museum, in part attributed to Shakespeare, and in part written in his own handwriting, a similar appeal against social injustice is made (in this case, the attacking of refugee foreigners):

Imagine that you see the wretched strangers,
Their babies at their backs, and their poor luggage,
Plodding to the ports and coasts for transportation …

Would you *be pleased*
To find a nation of such barbarous temper,
That, breaking out in hideous violence,
Would not afford you an abode on earth,
Whet their detested knives against your throats,
Spurn you like dogs, and like as if that God
Owed* not nor made you? What would you *think*
To be thus used? This is the strangers' case,
And this your Momtanish† inhumanity.

Both appeals belong to the climate of the Mermaid. For hand-in-hand with the Rosicrucian quest for the spirit behind matter went the quest for the spirit in man that strove towards a right social structure for the new age then dawning. One of the Rosicrucian aims in Shakespeare's day was "to heal the diseases of the society of its time".[24] And in *The Chymical Wedding*, those laborators who became Knights of the Golden Stone are pledged to work at the transmutation of the outer social life.

But if it took courage, in *A Midsummer Night's Dream*, to flout the Puritans by putting fairies on the stage, how much more did it take, in *The Merchant of Venice*, to flout the populace by holding up a mirror to man's inhumanity to man!

In the old Italian story which formed the framework of this play (it had appeared on 1558 in a collection called *Il Pecorone*), the heroine, the Lady Belmonte, is to be won by passing a test of wakefulness. This the hero, Gianetto, does and wins her. Meanwhile his godfather, Ansaldo, is unable to repay the ten thousand ducats he had borrowed from a Jew, and must forfeit the pound of flesh specified in the bond. The Lady of Belmonte, in the guise of doctor of laws, rescues him as Portia rescues Antonio. Even the episode of the rings at the conclusion

* Owned   †Mohammedanish
[24] Wigston: BACON, SHAKESPEARE AND THE ROSICRUCIANS

of the play appears also in this old story.

One feels it in one's bones that it was that one word, *Belmonte* – Beautiful Mountain – that opened the sluice-gates through which Shakespeare's exuberant creativeness poured Rosicrucian impulses into this play. In the picture-language of Rosicrucianism, as in that of myth and fairytale (and of all Holy Writ), a mountain is that part of earth which is nearest heaven. So in this name we have a radiant picture of a higher and purer consciousness placed over against the darker workaday one of the city of Venice, with Shylock's house as its nucleus of night. In the past, Man dwelt on the beautiful mountain; in the future, Man will dwell on it again. In the present, our everyday consciousness is a mercantile one, and the darkest spot in our industrial culture is ducat-worship, in whatever language and by whatever race.

It is as if the pageant-stage of the medieval Mystery-Cycles had been preserved into Elizabethan times solely for the presentation of this play, so felicitously and precisely does its convention of Heaven's Tower to the right, Hell's Mouth to the left, and Middle-Earth between lend itself to the picture of the countinghouse of Venice between Belmont and Shylock's house – Belmont out-flowing with light and music, open-handed and open-hearted, Shylock's house "dark as Erebus" and shuttered like the heart and hand of usury –

> *What! are there masques? Lock up my door ...*
> *And stop my house's ears, I mean my casements;*
> *Let not the sound of shallow foppery enter*
> *My sober house.*
>
> (II, v)

Jessica even voices this contrast of "hell" and "heaven". When Launcelot Gobbo comes to say farewell to her, she replies:

> *I am sorry thou wilt leave my father so:*
> *Our house is hell, and thou, a merry devil,*
> *Didst rob it of some taste of tediousness.*
>
> (II, iii)

And, having found a blissful haven in Belmont, she remarks to Lorenzo:

> *It is very meet*
> *The Lord Bassanio live an upright life,*
> *For, having such a blessing in his lady,*
> *He finds the joys of heaven here on earth.*
>
> (III, v)

Even the fact that the curtains of Heaven's Tower were still traditionally embroidered with moons and stars (there is a reference as late as 1594 to "a player's Heaven, distinguished with moon and stars") had a certain happy appropriateness; at Portia's lovely homecoming to a scene so saturated with moonlight that we realize we are transported back to Diana's realm, it is not only the floor of heaven that is inlaid with patines of bright gold, but also the embroidered walls of Belmont.

For in Belmont we are in a world of spiritual realities. Venice is but a rose's shadow; Shylock's house, alas, is but the shadow of that shadow; Belmont is the true rose. In Belmont everything speaks a different language from

its Venetian one. In Belmont gold is sun-like; it scatters
its bounty freely. Portia has gold in abundance, but she
holds it only to be of service to others.

In Venice, only Antonio uses gold as it is used in Belmont,
freely giving it for love of a friend; while for Shylock gold
has become the poison for the soul Romeo describes to
the apothecary from whom he buys poison for the body:

> *There is thy gold, worse poison to men's souls,*
> *Doing more murders in this loathsome world*
> *Than these poor compounds that you may not sell.*
> *I* sell *thee poison; thou hast sold me none.*
>
> *(Romeo and Juliet, V, i)*

So, when the Prince of Morocco chooses the golden
casket, with its inscription, "who chooseth me shall gain
what many men desire," he finds within, not the "angel
on a golden bed" of his surmises, but a skull. For, in
Belmont, to choose gold for its own sake is to choose
death. Gold is, as Bassanio observes, hard food for Midas.
In Belmont, the moon shines bright. Silver is its gentle
radiance, leading Lorenzo to penetrate and share with
Jessica the secret of the music of the spheres –

> *There's not the smallest orb which thou behold'st*
> *But in his motion like an angel sings,*
> *Still quiring to the young-eyed cherubins;*
> *Such harmony is in immortal souls.*
>
> *(V, i)*

In Venice, silver is trade's maid-of-all-work, a "pale and
common drudge 'tween man and man". Even the Duke

is prepared to sacrifice Antonio's life rather than abate the law,

> *Since that trade and profit of the city*
> *Consisteth of all nations.*
>
> *(III, iii)*

As the moon reflects the sun's light, so silver, the moon-metal, is also a mirror. Says the silver casket's scroll:

> *There be fools alive, I wis,*
> *Silver'd oer; and so was this.*
>
> *(II, ix)*

That is to say: the portrait you have found within is a reflection of your own true being.

So, when the Prince of Arragon chooses the silver casket, with its inscription, "who chooseth me shall get as much as he deserves," (on which he comments, "I will assume desert"), he finds, within, "the portrait of a blinking idiot". For who but a fool would dare to think in Belmont that he *deserved* the peerless Portia?

In the city of the plain, lead is a dull, heavy metal; coffins are made of it. There (for Venice is a kind of mineral world) deposits of its ore are richest where dis-integrating forces, such as strong lime deposits, occur. In Belmont (which is a plant-like world) it is the condensing forces of lead which harden the seed into a shrine for its tiny pulse of sun-life, its Portia portrait. On the beautiful mountain, lead has a Phoenix quality. "Who chooseth me must give and hazard all he hath," is inscribed on the leaden casket. Alchemy was able to change lead into

gold; and when Bassanio had given and hazarded all he
had, he found within the dead lead the radiant life, the
spiritual gold, of Portia.

The casket scenes take up more of the play than is
dramatically justifiable. This should already be an indication to us to pause and consider them deeply, since
Shakespeare evidently attaches profound importance to
them. As we muse on them it becomes clear that we are
being shown picture after picture of the difference between appearance and reality, between *Schein* and *Sein*.
Each suitor is told the same truth in different words.
Morocco, who chose the golden casket, finds written on
the scroll within it:

All that glitters is not gold.
Gilded tombs do worms infold.
(II, vii)

Arragon,who chose the silver casket, found written on
his scroll:

Some there be that shadows kiss;
Such have but a shadow's bliss.
(II, ix)

While Bassanio makes his choice, Portia bids music
sound –

Tell me, where is fancy bred,
Or in the heart, or in the head?

How begot, how nourishèd?

It is engender'd in the eyes,
With gazing fed; and fancy dies
In the cradle where it lies.

                              (III, ii)

The song recalls the *leit-motif* of *Love's Labour's Lost*: that
the attraction of the outer semblance, if it grows into
nothing deeper, is doomed to die; it is the love of the
heart, penetrating this disguise to find the inward secret,
the true rose, that lives.
It has been ingeniously suggested that Portia designed
the end-rhymes of the first three lines of the song to lead
Bassanio's mind to the right metal. To accept this would
surely be to flaw Portia's integrity. But that the meaning
of the song flowed straight into his own thought-stream
is evident from his immediate comment:

So may the outward shows be least themselves:
The world is still deceiv'd with ornament.

                              (III, ii)

And this, via a meandering soliloquy, leads him at last to:

But thou, thou meagre lead,
That rather threat'nest than doth promise aught,
Thy plainness moves me more than eloquence,
And here choose I.

                              (III, ii)

And *his* "gentle scroll", too, still dwells on the same
theme:

You that choose not by the view,
Chance as fair and choose as true!

(III, ii)

With this theme we find Shakespeare concerned again
and again. In *The Tempest*, the primitive souls of Trinculo
and Stephano are beguiled by the "stale and trumpery"
that waylay them outside Prospero's cell. In *Pericles* the
outer beauty of Antiochus' daughter masks her inner
loathliness; Dionyza's "black villainy" is likewise
masked for years by the "glittering golden characters" she
has set on Marina's tomb; the good Simonides, like
Bassanio, refuses to judge by "the view", and, when
Pericles appears at the tourney in rusty armour, comments
shrewdly:

Opinion's but a fool that makes us scan
The outward habit by the inward man.

(Pericles, II, ii)

When masks temporarily led the young men astray in
Love's Labour's Lost, it was part of their education by life;
but in *King Lear* we are to be shown how looking too long
on externals can plunge the soul into moral catastrophe.
Here, in *The Merchant of Venice*, to discriminate rightly
between appearance and reality is to take a step in
initiation. To pass the test of the caskets is to win not
only Portia's self but with her the lordship of her bright
kingdom –

Myself and what is mine to you and yours
In now converted: but now I was the lord

Of this fair mansion, master of my servants,
Queen o'er myself; and even now, but now,
This house, these servants, and this same myself
Are yours, my lord. I give them with this ring.

(III, ii)

For Portia is herself a picture of an attribute of man's higher self towards which, in the vanguard of evolution, the Rosicrucians were already striving – that purification of the feeling-life till it could lead to sense-free thinking and its vehicle shone like pure gold which in Greek mythology was known as the Golden Fleece. That Bassanio, mere fortune-hunter as he may appear in Venice, is, in his desire to unite with Portia, inwardly on a Jason-quest is indicated in his words to Antonio:

Her sunny locks
Hang on her temples like a golden fleece;
Which makes her seat of Belmont Colchos' strand,
And many Jasons come in quest of her.

(I, i)

We have said of Rosaline in *Love's Labour's Lost* that she stands like Berowne's guide into the realm of the Creative Word. In *The Merchant of Venice*, Portia stands like Bassanio's guide into this realm of the cleansed feeling-life – this realm which the alchemist sought to approach through a mystical apprehension of the salt-forming processes. And it is indeed, Alchemy, in the person of the Virgin, Alchimia, who, in *The Chymical Wedding*, is Portia's prototype.

In a castle set, like Belmont, on a mountain, Christian

Rosenkreutz is guided by Alchimia's torch; she is called
Virgo Lucifera, the Virgin Light-bearer. Portia also gives
light; Bassanio, on his homecoming with the reprieved
Antonio, greets her with:

> *We should hold day with the Antipodes,*
> *If you would walk in absence of the sun.*
>
> (V, i)

The very picture of Alchimia coming into the guest-hall
to the sound of more delicate music, robed in white,
sparkling with purest gold, lit by "many thousands of
lighted tapers, matching of themselves," has a tender
reflection in that of Portia returning, drawn home by
music, the moonlight sleeping sweetly on the bank, the
floor of heaven thick inlaid with patines of bright gold.
Alchimia sets the test by which the worthy wedding
guests are winnowed out from the unworthy. Each is
weighed, on great golden scales, against seven weights
which are the Seven Liberal Arts. Those who pass the
test are those who have used these arts as a path of
spiritual development; those who are found wanting are
those who have drawn from them only external erudi-
tion. Thus this test, like Portia's test of the three caskets,
is passed only by that soul which searches out the "inward
secret" and is not misled by "outward shows".
In both cases those who fail the tests must leave at once
and never reveal what has happened, while those who
entered the castle by fraud are dealt with much more
harshly.
Those guests who pass Alchimia's test are made Knights
of the Golden Fleece. Gratiano announces his friend
Bassanio's success in the same picture:

We are Jasons, we have won the fleece.
(III, ii)

When Christian Rosenkreutz is made keeper of the Gate, at the end of *The Chymical Wedding*, he is given a ring of office engraved with the word, *Constantia*, and is bidden to be faithful to his trust. At the end of *The Merchant of Venice* there is much surface merriment over Bassanio's and Gratiano's giving-away of the rings they had received with Portia's and Nerissa's hands –

BASSANIO:
                    Sweet Portia,
If you did know to whom I gave the ring,
If you did know for whom I gave the ring,
And would conceive for what I gave the ring,
When naught would be accepted but the ring –
PORTIA:
If you had known the virtue of the ring,
Or half her worthiness that gave the ring,
Or your own honour to contain the ring,
You would not then have parted with the ring
(V, i)

But to this light-hearted episode from *Il Pecorone* Shakespeare had brought a Mermaid meaning. When given the ring, Bassanio had vowed:

When this ring
Parts from my finger, then parts life from thence.
(III, ii)

And this was true in the deepest of senses, for with the

ring was bound up his union with Portia and his lordship over her realm. So now *Constantia* is re-engraved upon the relationship, and there is a solemn pledge in the quip with which Gratiano ends the play:

> *Well, while I live I'll fear no other thing*
> *So sore as keeping safe Nerissa's ring.*
>   (V, i)

When Bassanio approaches Antonia with his plan, "how to get clear of all the debts I owe," he does so in the idiom of Venice:

> *In my school-days, when I had lost a shaft,*
> *I shot his fellow of the self-same flight*
> *The self-same way with more advisèd watch,*
> *To find the other forth, and by adventuring both,*
> *I oft found both ... If you please*
> *To shoot another arrow that self way*
> *Which you did shoot the first, I do not doubt,*
> *As I will watch the aim, or to find both,*
> *Or bring your latter hazard back again,*
> *And thankfully rest debtor for the first.*
>   (I, i)

(Shakespeare must have heard this idiom often in his prosperous period; already as early as 1597, when the tide of his fortunes was only just turning, the boy-next-door of his childhood, Richard Quiney, now a London mercer, whose son Thomas was nineteen years later to marry Shakespeare's daughter Judith, writes to him: "Loving countryman, I make bold of you as a friend, craving your help with £30 upon Mr. Bushell's and my security. You shall friend me much on helping me out of all the debts I owe in London – I thank God – and, much quiet my mind, which would not be indebted.")

But when Bassanio hears of Antonio's danger, he acts as one acts in Belmont – prepared to give and hazard all, he leaves immediately, on his wedding-day, hastening to his friend's aid "with gold to pay the petty debt twenty times over". And Portia does even more – in her inspired plea for mercy she brings Belmont itself down into Venice, dropping like the gentle dew from heaven upon the place beneath.

In this play that plea is a seed which will only ripen in later ones. It spring spontaneously from Shakespeare's untried heart, which must pass through the bitterness of betrayal before it can transform it into the deliberate out-flowing virtue of Posthumous' deed of mercy towards Lachimo, who has so deeply wronged him and whose life is now in his hands:

> *The power that I have on you is to spare you;*
> *The malice towards you, to forgive you. Live,*
> *And deal with others better –*
>
> *(Cymbeline, V, v)*

and of Cymbeline's kingly amnesty, catching generous fire from Posthumus' example:

> *Nobly doomed!*
> *We'll learn our freeness of a son-in-law:*
> *Pardon's the word to all.*
>
> *(Cymbeline, V, v)*

It is Shylock's tragedy that he cannot rise to creative response to Portia's sun-filled plea. Already, in *Romeo and Juliet*, and with Hermia and Aegeus in *A Midsummer Night's Dream*, Shakespeare has indicated that the new conditions of the the new age demand a loosening of the constrictions of the blood-bond. Now, within the framework of quite different terms of reference, he indicates it again. Shylock cannot respond because the doctrine of an eye for an eye pulses in his blood-stream. He is, indeed, a prisoner of the racial forces in that blood-stream. Comment after comment show him grown rigid and caught fast in the fettering cocoon of race:

He hates our sacred nation ...
Sufferance is the badge of all our tribe.
(I, iii)

My own flesh and blood rebel ...
The curse never fell upon our nation till now.
(III, i)

His rejection of Bassanio's invitation to dine is a kind of archetypal gesture:

I will buy with you, sell with you, talk with you,
walk with you, but I will not eat with you,
drink with you, nor pray with you.
(I, iii)

For eating together, both in life and in ritual, is an act of community, bringing men together in freedom.

The terrible deed to which his blood drives him, his usury applauds:

> *I will have the heart of him, if he forfeit; for,*
> *were he out of Venice, I can make what*
> *merchandise I will.*
>
>   *(III, i)*

His merchant interests unite with the agonies of the rejected and the Old Covenant justice of an eye for eye to make him

> *A stony adversary, an inhuman wretch*
> *Uncapable of pity, void and empty*
> *From any dram of mercy.*
>
>   *(IV, i)*

And the sorrow of it is that inwardly, as well as outwardly, he loses the whole world. The Duke asks, despairing:

> *How shalt thou hope for mercy, rendering none?*
>
>   *(IV, i)*

And Gratiano shrewdly touches the heart of the tragedy:

> *Not on thy sole, but on thy soul, harsh Jew,*
> *Thou mak'st thy knife keen.*
>
>   *(III, i)*

In the matter of choosing a husband Portia is hedged about by the authority of the blood-bond:

> *The lottery of my destiny*
> *Bars me the right of voluntary choosing.*
>
> *(II, i)*

But its restriction sits easily on her because she wears it willingly. She jests about it to Nerissa:

> *So is the will of a living daughter curbed by*
> *the will of a dead father.*
>
> *(I, ii)*

But in the same conversation she declares firmly and solemnly:

> *If I live to be as old as Sibylla, I will die as*
> *chaste as Diana, unless I be obtained by*
> *the manner of my father's will.*
>
> *(I, ii)*

In other words, I *choose* to be governed by my father's will. Portia knows intuitively what our later age has to discover empirically – that to be free includes the freedom to obey. Everything is built upon her soul's free assent.

The Elizabethan era saw the last flaring and flowering of medieval ardours and Renaissance fevers. Soon was to come the Age of Reason, and, after it, the Age of Technology. Virtue changed its nature; it was no longer the antithesis of vice, but the walking of a tightrope between

two vices – that of the too much and that of the too little
of itself. In the new age just dawning, the badge of virtue
would be moderation.

It was not until Shakespeare had plumbed the depths and
heights of his own nature that he was able, in *Timon of
Athens*, to treat this aspect of our era on an epic scale; but
already in *The Merchant of Venice* it is present in his mind.
Thus Nerissa comments:

> *For aught I see, they are as sick that surfeit with
> too much as they that starve with nothing. It is
> no mean happiness, therefore, to be seated in the mean;
> superfluity comes sooner by white hairs, but competency
> lives longer.*
>
> (I, ii)

And when Bassanio chooses the right casket, Portia
exclaims, in a shaken aside:

> *O love! be moderate; allay thy ecstasy!
> In measure rain thy joy; scant this excess;
> I feel too much thy blessing; make it less,
> For fear I surfeit!*
>
> (III, ii)

As with the plea for mercy, so also the concept of the
golden mean is dropped into this play as a seed-idea to
be ripened later by Shakespeare's own life-experience.

The opening words of *The Merchant of Venice* are spoken
by Antonio:

In sooth, I know not why I am so sad:
It wearies me; you say it wearies you;
But how I caught it, found it, or came by it,
What stuff 'tis made of, whereof it is born,
I am to learn …
I hold the world but as the world, Gratiano:
A stage where every man must play a part,
and mine a sad one.

To which Gratiano retorts:

Why should a man, whose blood is warm within,
Sit like his grandsire, cut in alabaster?

(I, i)

Salanio also comments on Antonio's "embracèd heaviness". A new kind of man appears in him, of a nature which will become familiar to us in Jaques and Orsino – a man in whom, a streak of melancholy is inherent, who is an onlooker rather than a doer. This onlooker consciousness was to be a particular mark of the new man of the new age – our own age; and after these preliminary thumbnail sketches, Shakespeare's prophetic genius, as we will now see, painted a full-length portrait of the birth of this new consciousness, in Hamlet.

CHAPTER IX

HAMLET, PRINCE OF DENMARK

"But now a different drama is being acted;
For this once let me be.

Yet the order of the acts is planned,
And the end of the way inescapable.
I am alone; all drowns in the Pharisees'
    hypocrisy.
To live your life is not as simple as to
    cross a field."

BORIS PASTERNAK[25]

A S woman, Portia is Shakespeare's first living, breathing heroine. Who sat for her human portrait? Clearly neither Stratford farmer's daughter, nor Oxford tavernhostess, nor London merchant's wife; and although Shakespeare had played at Court and was on friendly terms with courtiers at the Mermaid, it was not customary in those days for an actor, who, however gifted and famed, still wore a servant's livery, to mix socially with cultured women.

Yet between *A Midsummer Night's Dream* and *The Merchant of Venice* such a woman had come into his life; and the group of comedies which follow embody a series of lovely girls, sparkling, witty, aristocratic, playfully free of speech, who might be sisters, yet each individual and exquisite in her own right – Beatrice, Viola, Rosalind, Olivia – each in love, yet each the spirit of comedy incarnate.

[25] HAMLET

Rosaline in *Love's Labour's Lost* is clearly a light pencil sketch of a court lady drawn from a little distance. The human aspect of Portia is that of Rosaline come alive.

This was the period of Shakespeare's love-affair with Mary Fitton; and it does not seem unreasonable to deduce that this bevy of bewitching sisters mirror her as she appeared to his enamoured poet's eye in the first ecstatic period of their relationship.

In *Much Ado about Nothing* (1598), the Duke acts as Claudio's messenger, wooing Hero on his behalf. *Twelfth Night* (1600) is again a story of messengers between lovers. In Shakespeare's own life at this point, Pembroke was acting as his liaison with his own Dark Lady.

Then, suddenly, there are no more bewitching sisters. In 1601, the year in which his long betrayal becomes past mending, Shakespeare shows in *Troilius and Cressida* a new bitter contempt for women. Unlike his Greek sources, he paints Cressida as untrue to Troilus, who, in his suffering, find himself – an unwitting prophecy of the eventual course of this parallel phase in Shakespeare's own soul-history.

But meanwhile he has suddenly to bear the catastrophic pangs of dispriz'd love. At the same time he loses, in the political upheavals, the protection of two good friends, Essex and Southampton, and is being subjected to the law's delay (and possibly also the insolence of office) in the matter of the Privy Council's Enquiry. All this when he has lately reached the age of thirty-five – that dread moment, when, in our era, the individual is laid bare to his own eyes. A man's first clear awareness of his own egohood entails great soul-loneliness; and Shakespeare, like a sensitively strung instrument, feels on his pulses every agony the new consciousness of selfhood can entail. New abysses of thought and experience open successively to him; and in 1602, as the first-fruits of all this, the being

of Hamlet is born.
Hamlet is strewn with traces of the scars of Shakespeare's betrayal:

> *Frailty, thy name is woman –*
>
> (I, ii)

> *If thou wilt needs marry, marry a fool; for wise men know well enough what monsters you make of them – God hath given you one face, and you make yourselves another: you jig, you amble, and you lisp, and nickname God's creatures, and make your wantonness your ignorance. Go to, I'll no more on't –*
>
> (III, i)

> OPHELIA: *'Tis brief, my lord.*
> HAMLET: *As woman's love –*
>
> (III, ii)

> *There lives within the very flame of love*
> *A kind of wick or snuff that will abate it.*
>
> (IV, xii)

And Hamlet's complaints in his famous soliloquy would seem to have more relevance to Shakespeare's own condition at that time than to that of a Prince of Denmark:

> *For who would bear the whips and scorns of time,*
> *The oppressor's wrong, the proud man's contumely,*
> *The pangs of dispriz'd love, the law's delay,*
> *The insolence of office, and the spurns*
> *That patient merit of the unworthy takes,*

When he himself might his quietus make
With a bare bodkin?

                                        (III, i)

These outer misfortunes pressed in upon a soul, already
ripe for a momentous change of consciousness which was
perhaps at that time understood only by the Rosicrucians.
They knew that a man living in the group-soul, but with
his own ego unawakened or still weak, was helpless before
life if detached from that group's encompassing support.
Man's new task was to develop the seed of his own
egohood, so that, standing alone in freedom, he could
make free decisions. A thoughtful study of history reveals
this gradual change, which even yet is not complete,
from men living entirely within the life-stream of their
tribe or family, to men beginning to free themselves from
the blood-tie and to stand alone, supported by their own
inner forces in the place of group custom and convention.
The success or failure of the ego is accomplishing this, or
some phase of the soul's history along this path, is one
aspect of the varied themes of all Shakespeare's tragedies.
His Romeo and Juliet, for example, conceive a passionate
individual love for one another although their families
are bitter enemies. Freeing themselves from the blood-
tie, they are true to their love, but at the cost of their
lives. In a beautiful conclusion, the sacrificed love of the
two young people reaches out from beyond the grave to
join the hands of their families in friendship:

PRINCE: *Capulet! Montague!*
See what a scourge is laid upon your hate,

That heaven finds means to kill your joys with love.
CAPULET: *O brother Montague! give me thy hand.*
MONTAGUE: *But I will give thee more:*
For I will raise her statue in pure gold.
CAPULET: *As rich shall Romeo by his lady lie;*
Poor sacrifices of our enmity!

(Romeo and Juliet, V, iii)

Discussing the change brought about in the soul-constitu-
tion of man by withdrawal from the group-soul, Rudolf
Steiner[26] contrasts Hector and Hamlet – the former a
strong, vigorous and co-ordinated personality, a man of
wide humanity, with a tender love for wife and child,
supported by being embedded in devotion to his family
and to his ancient city, Troy; the latter capable of being
as strong and vigorous and of as deep and tender a love,
but thrown off his balance by being stripped by circumstance of the support of family and group and compelled
to stand alone when his ego is not yet sufficiently mature
for such a test, so that he becomes a sceptic, a waverer,
one who cannot any longer find or fill his place in life.
One could almost say that in the opening scenes of the
play, Hamlet is in a state of suspended shock. Every soul,
to achieve self-consciousness, must be becalmed – with-
drawn and unresponsive to incentives to outer action
while, in a deaf and dumb creative pause, the inner
awakening takes place. And Hamlet, in addition, is
caught between past and future. His old nature, passionate and active, lives on in him out of the past; his con-
templative thought, an attribute of the future, constantly
paralyses his will and renders him unsure and irresolute.
So he stands bewildered before the questions: What is a
man? How stand I then? What is the truth of what
appears before me? What is the relation between this

[26] THE GOSPEL OF ST. MARK

outward seeming and its inner reality? – an intensifica-
tion of the questions of the Scholastics, no longer asked
in the quietness of a monastic cell but amid the harrowing
exigencies of a crisis in both inner and outer life.
Before what his uncle called Hamlet's transformation, he
had written to Ophelia:

> *Doubt thou the stars are fire;*
>   *Doubt thou the sun doth move;*
> *Doubt truth to be a liar;*
>   *But never doubt I love.*
>
>   *(II, ii)*

But now he has been expelled from that Ptolemaic Creation not merely into a Copernican but, darker yet, into
a Newtonian one. The majestical roof fretted with golden
fire now appears a foul and pestilent congregation of
vapours, this goodly frame, the earth, a sterile promontory. Man, the beauty of the world, the paragon of
animals, has become a quintessence of dust. And when
there is something so rotten in the state of Denmark then
even in his formerly revered mother evil lurks under the
appearance of good, how can he do other than doubt
truth to be a liar; how can he do other than doubt if he
himself still loves?
So the disparity between appearance and reality of the
earlier plays re-emerges in a new, more urgent form.
In these earlier plays there had been an outside commentator to explain to the central characters what was
happening within them – such, for example, as Friar
Lawrence in *Romeo and Juliet*. But now, as with the Furies
in Orestes, the outer has become inner. With Hamlet the
commentator is a hitherto unmet stranger lurking within
his own being, whose reportings strip the veil from his

own soul and bring about an inner conflict that threatens
to tear it apart.
This inner spectator puts an unerring finger on the condition of that soul whose rib he is:

> *Thus conscience* doth make cowards of us all;*
> *And thus the native hue of resolution*
> *Is sicklied o'er with the pale cast of thought,*
> *And enterprises of great pith and moment*
> *With this regard their currents turn awry,*
> *And lose the name of action.*
>
> *(III, i)*

Equally perspicacious can be his penetration of other
people, as when Hamlet remarks of Polonius:

> *That great baby you see there is not*
> *yet out of his swaddling clouts.*
>
> *(II, ii)*

For Polonius is still deeply swaddled in the blood-bond.
For this very reason he can, amid much trite and tedious
maundering, from time to time produce pearls handed
down out of ancient wisdom, such as:

> *To thine own self be true,*
> *And it must follow, as the night the day,*
> *Thou can'st not then be false to any man.*
>
> *(I, iii)*

But to do this one has either to have the swaddling

---

* consciousness

support of a blood-group canon of morality, or one has to
have an ego-directed self of one's own to be true to.
Laertes has the former; but Hamlet, jettisoned out of the
one, has not yet found home in the other.

The new-born ego-consciousness is isolated on three
levels – it is cut off from the surrounding world, from
unreflective action, and from the earlier interweaving
with fellow human beings. On all three levels it looks on
from without. Thus is becomes something entirely new in
man's soul-history – the spectator consciousness, the
onlooker we have already met in embryo in Antonio,
Jaques, Orsino.
"We are today so accustomed to the 'spectator' attitude
to life, the looking at the world completely outside us to
which we feel we do not essentially belong, that it is
difficult for us to realise that in *Hamlet* Shakespeare is
mediating a new type of consciousness into human experience. It is a consciousness that is localised in the
brain and nerves.
… The intellectual consciousness of the head brings with
it an exactness of thinking about the external world and
an accuracy of perception of that world unknown to
other modes of consciousness. But it does so by separating
the observer from the object."[27]
With every human quality there comes a point in time
when man is ripe to develop it inwardly of his own freewill. We saw in Chapter I, for example, the very moment
in history when external Furies became internal conscience.
Before the seed of any self-born faculty is thus sown in
human nature, it comes to a first flowering in some great
pioneer, whose heirs we may with gratitude count ourselves, since it is he who bequeathes to posterity the

[27] A.C. Harwood: SHAKESPEARE'S PROPHETIC MIND

organ he has fashioned (often, like Prometheus, with suffering) for the functioning of the new faculty.

Just as logical thought as a personal capacity first flowered in Artistotle; and the organ of compassion was first fashioned by Gautama Buddha; and Pythagoras' teacher, Pherekydes of Syros, was the first to think in concepts instead of in the pictures of the ancients; so we see Hamlet bearing the birth-pangs of the ego and the changeover from the participating consciousness of earlier times to the separative consciousness of our own.

Because it was England's destiny to blaze the trail to our modern material culture, the spectator-consciousness is particularly fully developed in the English people. Every Englishman, as Novalis observed, is an island (Who else discusses or argues with his hands in his pockets?) Even the name of the first English newspaper – *The Spectator* – is symptomatic.

"Shakespeare's *Hamlet* is to be regarded as a characteristic expression of the British folk-soul, and one of its mightiest manifestations ... English Philosophy – and this can be shown particularly well in the work of John Stuart Mill – is the philosophy of an *onlooker* ... The British folk-soul tends in all its activities to turn man into an onlooker; he stands outside phenomena; he looks at them as it were from the body. Shakespeare's greatness consists particularly in his capacity for standing at a distance and watching life objectively."[28]

One sees then a certain truth in Professor Bradley's observation that, of all Shakespeare's characters, only Hamlet could have written Shakespeare's plays.

Professor Dover Wilson has ingeniously pointed out that, at one point in *Hamlet*, spectatorship is three-deep. Before the play within the play, introduced by Hamlet to test the guilt of the King, the players first perform the action

[28] Rudolf Steiner: THE SOUL OF THE PEOPLE

in dumbshow. Thus the audience need not watch the
play itself; they know the gist of it and can concentrate
on watching Hamlet, who is watching the King, who is
watching the play.

Before his father's death, Hamlet was a student at
Wittenberg, thirty years old – old for a student in those
days, but there is evidence that Shakespeare had originally meant him to be a youth of nineteen. Doubtless he
felt, on consideration, that so young a soul would be too
slight a vessel for all that it must carry. Doubtless, too,
he had Mermaid intimations, as well as those of his own
soul's experience, of the age at which a man was ripe for
such experience.
Hamlet's greeting of his two fellow-students suggests that
he had formerly been of a cheerful disposition and a
pleasant boon-companion:

My excellent good friends! How dost thou,Guildenstern?
Ah, Rosencrantz! Good lads, how do ye both?
                         (II, ii)

Ophelia describes that earlier Hamlet thus:

The courtier's, scholar's, soldier's, eye, tongue, sword;
The expectancy and rose of the fair state,
The glass of fashion and the mould of form,
The observed of all observers.
                         (III, i)

He seems to have been accomplished in all customary
"arts and exercises", and longs to pit himself against

another master-fencer in Laertes. He was embedded in
the security of his parents' love and the affection of both
court and country for the admired young heir-apparent.
But now the strokes off destiny fall. His beloved father
dies mysteriously, and within two months his mother is
married to his uncle. Suddenly the uncle is on the throne,
Hamlet is passed over. He stands bewildered and alone,
his fledgling ego unequal to the situation. He falls into a
vein of melancholy:

> *How weary, stale, flat and unprofitable*
> *Seem to me all the uses of this world.*
> *(I, ii)*

From his dead father's ghost he learns that his uncle
murdered him:

> HAMLET:
> *Speak: I am bound to hear.*
> GHOST:
> *So art thou to revenge …*
> *If thou didst ever thy dear father love,*
> *Revenge his foul and most unnatural murder.*
> HAMLET:
> *Haste me to know't, that I with wings as swift*
> *As meditation or the thoughts of love*
> *May sweep to my revenge …*
> *Thy commandment all alone shall live*
> *Within the book and volume of my brain.*
> *(I, v)*

But he has been rudely jarred loose of the blood-bond.

Like Shylock's blood, Hamlet's blood in the shape of his
father's ghost cries, Revenge! But something that has
been freed from the blood-bond holds him back. What
would, under the old dispensation, have been "excitements of my reason and my blood" are now incitements
only of the latter. The book and volume of his brain is
the very place in which the ghost's commandment can
no longer live.

A man cast in the mould of an earlier day could have
fulfilled his oath within an hour of its inception. A man
of the future whose higher ego was shining into his soul,
such as Posthumus or Prospero, could replace revenge by
forgiveness. Where the past and the future meet in him,
Hamlet is torn apart:

> *The time is out of joint; O cursed spite,*
> *That ever I was born to set it right!*
> > *(I, v)*

In arresting contrast, the instantaneousness of Laertes'
reaction to the news of his fathers's death comes straight
out of the past:

> *That drop of blood that's calm proclaims me bastard ...*
> > *I'll be revenged*
> *Most throughly for my father.*
> > *(IV, v)*

And so he is. For him the end justifies even a poisoned
rapier. Hamlet reproaches himself:

> *I am pigeon-liver'd, and lack gall*

To make oppression bitter, or ere this
I should have fatted all the region kites
With this slave's offal.
(II, ii)

But a new doubt has come:

The spirit I have seen

May be the devil. I'll have grounds
More relative than this: the play's the thing
Wherein I'll catch the conscience of the king.
(II, ii)

The play, which, with a flash of his former wit, Hamlet calls *The Mouse-trap*, does catch the conscience of the king. The blood makes its claim again:

Now could I drink hot blood,

And so such bitter business as the day
Would quake to look on.
(III, ii)

But when the opportunity presents itself to kill the king at prayer, the intellect once more falls to refining:

Am I then reveng'd,

To take him in the purging of his soul,
When he is fit and season'd for his passage?
No.
(III, iii)

Hamlet's vacillation at this point takes a toll of seven

other lives – Polonius, whom he kills as he lurks behind
the arras ("I took thee for thy better"); the docile
Ophelia, who, at her father's death, loses her reason and
is drowned; Guildenstern and Rosencrantz, slain by the
King of England at the request of the letter Hamlet sends
him in place of his uncle's orders to have Hamlet killed;
the Queen, who drinks of the poisoned cup his uncle had
prepared for Hamlet; Laertes and Hamlet himself, who
are both slain by one poisoned rapier.
When the Ghost returns, Hamlet asks:

> *Do you not come your tardy son to chide?*
>
> *(III, iv)*

Yet even "this visitation" does not whet his "blunted
purpose"; he allows his uncle to send him to England
with Guildenstern and Rosecrantz. His meeting with
Fortinbras, Prince of Norway, marching to a senseless
war against the Polacks, rouses his admiration of the
former's determined purpose, in such contrast with his
own procrastination:

> *Sure, he that made us with such large discourse,*
> *Looking before and after, gave us not*
> *That capability and god-like reason*
> *To fust in us unus'd. Now, whe'r it be*
> *Bestial oblivion, or some craven scruple*
> *Of thinking too precisely on the event,*
> *A thought, which, quarter'd, hath but one part wisdom*
> *And ever three parts coward, I do not know*
> *Why yet I live to say "This thing's to do",*
> *Sith I have cause and will and strength and means*
> *To do't.*
>
> *(IV, iv)*

This is exactly true. He does not understand his own fumbling attempts to use god-like reason in a new god-like way. He does not understand himself, struggling as he is to give birth to the ego that can make free decisions out of its own strength.

On the voyage outer circumstance forces him into swift and resolute action. Having boarded the pirates' vessel alone, he has himself taken back to Denmark. But once there, he begins thinking too precisely on the event again. He reminds Horatio:

> *In my heart there was a kind of fighting*
> *That would not let me sleep ... Is't not to be damned*
> *To let this canker of our nature come*
> *In further evil?*
>
> *(V, ii)*

Laertes he warns, as they struggle together in Ophelia's grave:

> *Though I am not splenetive and rash,*
> *Yet have I in me something dangerous.*
>
> *(V, i)*

He accepts without any suspicion of foul play the fencing-match with Laertes arranged by the king. But he tells Horatio:

> *Thou wouldst not think how ill all's here about*
> *my heart ... such a kind of gain-giving**
> *as would perhaps trouble a woman.*

---

* misgiving

HORATIO:
If your mind dislike anything, obey it.
I will say you are not fit.
HAMLET:
We defy augury; there's a special providence
in the fall of a sparrow. If it be now, 'tis not to come;
if it be not to come, 'twill not be now; if it be not now,
yet it will come; the readiness is all.

(V, ii)

It *is* now. Laertes wounds Hamlet with the poisoned
rapier; then, in scuffling, they change rapiers, and Hamlet
wounds Laertes. Laertes, dying, warns him:

Hamlet, thou art slain.
No medicine in the world can do thee good;
In thee there is not half an hour of life.
The treacherous instrument is in thy hand,
Unbated and envenom'd. The king, the king's to blame.

(V, ii)

And at long last Hamlet moves:

Then, venom, do thy work!

And, dying, he stabs the King. "Hamlet achieves action
only at the moment of death."[29]
The King, the Queen, Hamlet, Laertes lie dead. Young
Fortinbras of Norway will be King of Denmark.
But Horatio still lives, Horatio, to whom Hamlet said:

[29] A.C. Harwood: SHAKESPEARE'S PROPHETIC MIND

Thou hast been
As one, in suffering all, that suffers nothing,
A man that fortune's buffets and rewards
Hast ta' en with equal thanks; and bless'd are those
Whose blood and judgement are so well co-mingled
That they are not a pipe for fortune's finger
To sound what stop she please. Give me that man
That is not passion's slave, and I will wear him
In my heart's core, ay, in my heart of heart,
As I do thee.

(III, ii)

This is the balance, this balance of blood and judgement, to which Hamlet has aspired, which he has not achieved, but which he recognizes as a noble picture of man. The picture in Act V of himself standing in a grave-yard, holding a skull in his hand, is like a picture of the new consciousness, seated no longer in the heart but in the head, and of the preoccupation with death which colours the whole play, so that Hamlet's traditional black costume is based on a reality. "There has been much throwing about of brains," says Guildenstern; and Hamlet asks:

What should such fellows as I do crawling
between heaven and earth?

(III, ii)

Such fellows bear the birthpangs of the ego, that there may be more Horatios in the world.

In *King Lear* we shall now see portrayed the death-pangs of that form of consciousness which had to die in order that this ego might be born.

CHAPTER X

KING LEAR

> "Think of a work of art, a tragedy. It can only arise if the poet's soul opens wide, goes out of itself, and learns to feel another's pain, to lay the burden of a stranger's suffering on his own soul. One understands the life of another through nothing so much as by taking upon one's own soul the burden of his pain".
>
> RUDOLF STEINER[30]

KING LEAR is universally regarded as Shakespeare's greatest achievement, though not his greatest play. Its cosmic proportions cannot be contained in the nutshell of a stage, even the imaginatively unbounded Elizabethan stage. Its storm is a world-storm, in which the very heavens themselves cry havoc; how then can mock thunder be other than travesty? And, like its churning "winds and persecutions of the sky," Lear's own passions and agonies are couched in imaginative pictures too mighty for physical portrayal.

At the heart of it all looms Lear, a giant figure, monstrously larger than life.

The gradual diminishing of parental authority as today's child achieves adolescence is a miniature echo of something which happened on a racial scale earlier in the

[30] THE ORIGIN OF SUFFERING

history of mankind. There was a time when Patriarchs, then Judges, then Kings, were the heaven-inspired guides and guardians of their peoples. Through their father-forces each group-soul led its tribe or race along its own predestined path.

The coming of the ego demanded a loosening and with-drawal of this guidance and guardianship. Each indi-vidual ego had to learn to be its own arbiter; while learning, it was free, like the Prodigal Son, even to go astray. The time of the kindly coercion of the blood was past.

Any force or impulse, however good and proper in its own time and place, becomes, if it outlives its rightful use and purpose, a power for evil. If the kindly coercion of the blood refused to abdicate when its time was past, it became tyrannous; its former natural support became unnatural fetters. "We have Abraham to our father," said the Pharisees even in the time of Christ. "To you your father should be as a god," says Theseus to Hermia in *A Midsummer Night's Dream*.

Lear is such a non-abdicating father-figure. He is an individual human being, but he is also at the same time something more – he is the prototypal patriarch. His individual destiny is therefore also a picture of a universal destiny. The cataclysms which result from his clinging to the power and trappings of his office while renouncing its responsibilities body forth the greater cataclysms of the patriarchal consciousness itself living on beyond its time and falling into decadence. So Shakespeare portrays him larger than life; for he *is* larger than himself.

In the opening scene of the play, Lear enters in all the glory of kingship. His courtiers and his children pay him homage. Yet we are shown at once that his powers of

judgement are feeble. He regards both Albany and Cornwall as his "beloved sons", though one is weak and the
other brutal; he greedily accepts the fulsome love-
speeches of his two elder daughters, and deprives Cordelia
of her dowry because she cannot heave her heart into her
mouth; he banishes Kent, the only courtier courageous
enough to tell him that in doing this he has done wrong.
To Lear's question, "Which of you shall we say doth love
us most?", Cordelia, disgusted by her sisters' insincerities,
replies:

> *I love your majesty*
> *According to my bond; nor more, nor less …*
> *You have begot me, bred me, lov'd me; I*
> *Return those duties back as are right fit,*
> *Obey you, love you, and most honour you.*
> *Why have my sisters husbands if they say*
> *They love you all? Haply, when I shall wed,*
> *That Lord whose hand must take my plight shall carry*
> *Half my love with him, half my care and duty:*
> *Sure I shall never marry like my sisters,*
> *To love my father all.*
>
> (I, i)

Here speaks the voice of the ego – the young ego, that
has not yet learnt tenderness and tact. Cordelia at this
stage is a little like our young today – conscious of
selfhood but unbending, undemonstrative, a little crude;
loving, true and "with washed eyes", but as yet still hard
and inarticulate.

In a purely patriarchal society the heart was the arena
of a love that was both a natural force and a commandment within the blood. In the age of developing individu-

ality such love within the blood-group still remained as
something instinctive, but there also became possible
love between two egos outside the blood-group, given
and received out of their own choice and freedom. When
Cordelia speaks of loving her father according to her
bond and reserving half her love for her husband, she is
expressing this evolutionary fact with the utmost clarity.
Though Lear cannot, Cordelia's suitor, the King of
France, immediately recognizes her "sin" as merely "a
tardiness in nature which oft leaves the history unspoke
that it intends to do", and joyfully bears her away,
dowerless as she is, to become "queen of us, of ours, and
our fair France".

That Lear, in dividing his kingdom between his daughters, proposed to retain it, and merely "to shake all care
and business from our age", is clear from his bestowal
of a coronet on each son-in-law while still retaining his
own crown. For his daughters are still, in his eyes, but
parts of his own being –

> *Filial ingratitude!*
> *Is it not as if this mouth should tear this hand*
> *For lifting food to it?*
>
> (III, iv)

Before men became separate, self-aware, ego-endowed
individuals, they had been unselfconscious organs of an
all-pervading, all-uniting group-soul; so that the image
Lear uses here is an exact imagination of the relationship
as it still appeared to his now atavistic consciousness.

He has a rude awakening when, installed in Goneril's
home, he asks one of her attendants, "Who am I, sir?"
and receives the reply, "My lady's father." The curse he

thereupon calls down on Goneril appears fantastically disproportionate to this reversal of importance unless one recognizes that to Lear it flouts what is to him a still Divine dispensation:

> *Hear, Nature, hear! dear goddess, hear!*
> *Suspend thy purpose if thou didst intend*
> *To make this creature fruitful!*
> *Into her womb convey sterility!*
> *Dry up in her the organs of increase,*
> *And from her derogate body never spring*
> *A babe to honour her! ... I have another daughter,*
> *Who, I am sure, is kind and comfortable.*
>
> *(I, iv)*

But when he goes to her, he finds himself shut out into the storm.

And now it seems to him not enough that Goneril alone should be unfruitiful, but that the whole evil race of mankind should die out:

> *Blow, winds, and crack your cheeks! rage! blow!*
> *You cataracts and hurricanes, spout*
> *Till you have drench'd our steeples, drown'd the cocks!*
> *You sulphurous and thought-executing fires,*
> *Vaunt-couriers to oak-cleaving thunderbolts,*
> *Singe my white head! And thou, all-shaking thunder,*
> *Strike flat the thick rotundity o' the world!*
> *Crack nature's moulds, all germens spill at once*
> *That make ingrateful man!*
>
> *(III, ii)*

The alchemists were aware of the inner connection of

storm and tempest with the untamed passions in man;
and in this storm on the heath it is as if Lear is finding
release from his pent-up atavistic Nature-forces, so that
through this shattering experience he shrinks to human
size and becomes aware of himself as "a poor, infirm,
weak and despis'd old man".
Now, for the first time, he thinks of others, saying to his
Fool, as they take refuge in as hovel:

"In, boy, go first!"

And then:

> *Poor naked wretches, wheresoe'er you are,*
> *That bide the pelting of this pitiless storm,*
> *How shall your houseless heads and unfed sides,*
> *Your loop'd and window'd raggedness, defend you*
> *From seasons such as these? O, I have ta'en*
> *Too little care of this. Take physic, pomp;*
> *Expose thyself to feel what wretches feel,*
> *That thou mayst shake the superflux to them,*
> *And show the heavens more just.*
>
> (III, iv)

It is through our own sufferings that our hearts open to
live over into the sufferings of others. Through his own
recent trials of the soul Shakespeare has come to compassion, and is able to bring Lear to it also through his.
Through its awakening in Lear of awe, compassion and
conscience, we see the threefold mission of Drama at
work in this storm on the heath.

In a sub-plot which echoes the main one, Gloucester re-enacts on a human level the superhuman tragedy of Lear. He banishes his faithful son Edgar, and trusts his traitorous bastard Edmund, who brings him into the power of the savage Cornwall, by whom, in a scene too agonising for the stage, Gloucester's eyes are put out. Edgar cares for his blinded father tenderly till the latter dies. Meanwhile Edmund, Goneril and Regan march with their troops against Cordelia, who has landed with an army to come to Lear's aid. The whole kingdom is in chaos.

All human relationships break down, the elements take over; Nature, too, becomes an enemy. The interweaving of the two identical plots gives the impression of a universal devastation; we stand before the ruins of a world. One feels that Shakespeare means very seriously the words spoken by a horrified Albany to his wife Goneril:

> *What have you done?*
> *Tigers, not daughters, what have you perform'd?…*
> *If that the heavens do not their visible spirits*
> *Send quickly down to tame these vile offences,*
> *It will come,*
> *Humanity must perforce prey on itself,*
> *Like monsters of the deep.*
>
> (IV, ii)

Lear is finally brought to Cordelia's camp; there, in skilled hands, and by the aid of music, he recovers his sanity. In all Shakespeare's plays there are few more tender and moving scenes than that of Lear's awakening and finding Cordelia beside him:

LEAR: *You do me wrong to take me out o' the grave;*
          Thou art a soul in bliss.
CORDELIA: *Sir, do you not know me?*
LEAR: *You are a spirit, I know; when did you die?*
CORDELIA: *Still, still far too wide.*
LEAR: *I am mightily abus'd. I should even die with*
                                                    pity
          To see another thus.
CORDELIA: *O! look upon me, sir,*
          And hold your hands in benediction o'er me:
          No, sir, you must not kneel.
LEAR: *Pray, do not mock me:*
          I am a very foolish fond old man,
          Fourscore and upward; and, to deal plainly,
          I fear I am not in my perfect mind ...
                          Do not laugh at me;
          For, as I am a man, I think this lady
          To be my child Cordelia.
CORDELIA: *And so I am, I am.*
LEAR: *Be your tears wet?*
          Yes, faith, I pray, weep not.
          If you have poison for me, I will drink it.
          I know you do not love me; for your sisters
          Have, as I do remember, done me wrong:
          You have some cause, they have not.
CORDELIA: *No cause, no cause.*
                        (IV, vii)

It took a very great soul indeed to achieve such an act of self-recognition as Lear had achieved in the storm. Now again we glimpse the greatness of the being who tries to kneel, in penitence and humility, before the daughter he had cast off. We glimpse, too, the mellowing of Cordelia's whole being, shaken to the depths and able now to express her tenderness for the father she had always deeply loved, though formerly in silence.

And now the massed forces of evil, led by Edmund, stand arrayed against Cordelia. She is defeated and taken prisoner; Lear is taken prisoner with her.
Lear has undergone a complete catharsis. His mind was formerly filled with pictures of beasts of prey; he had penetrated, in his passions and his agonies, to those lowest depths of the soul where monsters dwell; all hideous forms of bestial life had writhed through his consciousness. Now he speaks only of birds and butterflies, denizens of the air. His spirit, like them, is hovering above the harsh realities of the earth below; he and his beloved one will look down from above and

> Take upon's the mysteries of things
> As if we were God's spies.
>
> *(V, iii)*

Cordelia is anxious to meet "these sisters and these daughters" face to face. Lear wants only to be with her within the shelter of the prison walls.

> Come, let's away to prison;
> We two alone will sing like birds i' the cage ...
> Upon such sacrifices, my Cordelia,
> The gods themselves throw incense.
> He that parts us shall bring a brand from heaven,
> And fire us hence like foxes.
>
> *(V, iii)*

The brand that is to part is already on its way, and

not from heaven but from hell. Meanwhile Regan and Goneril are both consumed with lust for Edmund, who contracts himself to them both. The jealous sisters quarrel over him; Goneril poisons Regan and plunges a knife into her own heart.

Albany arrests Edmund on capital treason; Edgar, disguised, challenges his half-brother to single combat and mortally wounds him. Edmund cries:

> *Some good I mean to do*
> *Despite of mine own nature. Quickly send,*
> *Be brief in it to the castle … Take my sword,*
> *Give it to the captain. He hath commission*
> *To hang Cordelia in the prison, and*
> *To lay the blame upon her own despair.*
>
> *(V, iii)*

Edmund repents too late. Lear enters with Cordelia dead in his arms.

Many of Shakespeare's plays contain an arresting picture which is in each case central to its theme – one could almost call it an archetypal picture. In *Hamlet* it is that of the young prince standing in the grave-yard, skull in hand. In King Lear it is that of the old king bearing the dead Cordelia in his arms.

It echoes the picture in Eschenbach's *Parsifal*, of Sigune with her bridegroom, Schionatulander, lying slain upon her lap; and Michaelangelo's sculpture of the Pieta, with Mary bearing in her arms the body of the her dead Son. This is the high moment of Lear's path of purification. In him the patriarchal blood-love has completely abdicated in favour of the love given in freewill by ego to ego. In this last dire battle between group-soul of the past and

ego of the future, Cordelia has been slain by the machie-
vel who is the cold caricature of the latter. Lear's heart
bursts with grief. But in his own last words –

> *Look on her, look, her lips,*
> *Look there! look there!*
>
> *(V, iii)*

and in Edgar's

> *Look up, my lord!*

there breathes a delicate innuendo that the grave has no
final victory.

The old play of *King Leir* on which Shakespeare based
his own had a happy ending. In it Cordelia's forces won,
and Leir was restored to his throne. But Lear cannot be
restored. He has finally abdicated; the father-figure is
gone; he himself, in dying to the past has found his way
into the future. It is a happy ending of a sublimer sort.

Cordelia and Edmund are the only modern people in the
play – in different ways, each is an ego-being.
It it enlightening to compare Cordelia, Edmund, Hamlet
and Horatio in their relationship to the ego. Man, having
found himself, has to stand fast in his own integrity.
Hamlet is not yet able to do this. Cordelia grows into
doing it. Horatio does it without effort. Edmund does
not even try to do it; he stands fast instead in his own
self-seeking.
Horatio is steady and solid; he grows naturally into the

ego, quietly and without upheaval. Hamlet is all upheaval. Cordelia mellows out of the young ego's crudities
into a warm, gracious and compassionate human being.
Edmund is as inwardly cold as he is outwardly ravening;
his early-developed independent will, estranged from all
moral impulses, can work only destructively.

The new separative consciousness whose birth we saw in
Hamlet we have seen in *King Lear* taken further in two
directions – in Edmund a grim foreshadowing of what
happens when the icy head is in full control and the
warm heart takes no part in man's thinking and doing;
in Cordelia, thinking and feeling both active and under
the control of the ego, learning through suffering to live
over again into others – in itself already a preparation
for a new participating consciousness to be achieved prophetically in the final plays.

In the last two lines of the play, Shakespeare gives Lear
a noble epitaph:

> *The oldest hath borne most; we that are young*
> *Shall never see so much, nor live so long.*
> (V, iii)

The father-figure is dead; there is no fully-fledged ego-
being left alive to succeed him. Who is to be Britain's
transitional king?

Albany looks before and after, he begs the old Kent and
the young Edgar:

> *Friends of my soul, you twain,*
> *Rule in this realm, and the gor'd state sustain.*
> (V, iii)

But Kent replies that he has a journey shortly to go, to join his master, Lear. So this leaves only Edgar.

Edgar has been throughout the play a champion of the right. In that his father banished him he has a certain correspondence to Cordelia. When we first met him he was open-hearted and true, but credulous. Through all the experiences and sufferings life has since brought him he has grown in stature till he is able to say, not as Hamlet said, "The readiness is all," but "Ripeness is all." Edgar will make a good king; but his relationship is built on the *death* of evil, not on its regeneration.

Shakespeare, like all Initiates, had to plumb the heights and paths of human experience, and to do this as and when he was ripe for them. His plays are reflections of his own soul's history; they are expressions of stages in his own personal path of evolution. Each play explores some deeply significant riddle of existence in a quite new way, and this question of the regeneration rather than the death of evil we shall now see him tentatively exploring in *Pericles*.

CHAPTER XI

PERICLES, PRINCE OF TYRE

"This is that gentle heat that brooded on the waters and in six days hatched the world; this is that irradiation that dispels the clouds of sorrow and despair, and preserves the mind in serenity. Whosoever feels not the warm gale and gentle ventilation of this Spirit, though I feel his pulse I dare not say he lives; for truly, without this there is no heat under the Tropick, nor any light though I dwelt in the body of the Sun".

SIR THOMAS BROWNE[31]

WHEN Lear enters with Cordelia in his arms, Kent cries:

Is this the promised end?
(King Lear, V, iii)

It is not. It is a picture of world-catastrophe; all is reduced to chaos. But as the grain of wheat must be reduced to chaos before a new plant can germinate, so only out of chaos can a new cosmos be born.

Lear has looked into an abyss, and beasts have risen out of it to confront him. Before a new cosmos can be born, Shakespeare has to confront the beasts which rise out of his own.

With Cleopatra, is he perhaps purging his soul of a sickness still left lingering on it by his own dark lady? Is there a personal relevance in Antony's

[31] RELIGIO MEDICI

These strong Egyptian fetters I must break
Or lose myself in dotage?

(Antony and Cleopatra, I, ii)

In Coriolanus, is he perhaps probing a pride with which
his own marches? In Timon of Athens, is he holding up
the mirror to a lack moderation in his own nature and
marking how an excess even of liberality can produce a
pack of parasites and a savage misanthrope?

The ancients said that all things lead to a Mystery (*omnia
abeunt in mysterium*). When, following these three plays,
Shakespeare gives us *Pericles*, we are immediately aware
that he has passed some kind of Threshold. For there
now begins to sound the authentic note of the traveller
in new realms.

Pericles was based on a fifth century Greek story, *Apol-
lonius of Tyre*, which was translated into a wide variety
of medieval European languages. Chaucer's contemporary, Gower, retells it in narrative verse in 1390 in his
Confessio Amantis, which would seem to have been Shakespeare's immediate source, since "Gower as Chorus"
appears among the Dramatis Personae, his function being
to introduce each Act and comment on the Dumb Shows
interspersed through the play.

So startling is the sea-change suffered in this play by
Shakespeare's art as dramatist, so uneven is its language,
so flouted are the unities, so roving is its action (*Scene*
is given as "dispersedly in various countries"), that it
has been suspected of being an early play refurbished,
or, if indeed first written in maturity, to have been in
part the work of lesser collaborators. At the same time,
the sea-change is in other directions into something so
rich and strange portrayed in such a musical sequence of

pictures that as one reads it the conviction arises that Shakespeare has broken through into a new realm, that he is thinking now in precepts, that in him fantasy has been uplifted into imagination, that what he is writing is not an Elizabethan stage play but a timeless Mystery-drama.

Like all true Mystery-dramas, *Pericles* moves on two levels. On one it depicts a series of outer adventures. On another these outer adventures image forth some of those trials and tribulations the soul must suffer on its path of inner development. And perhaps we shall find ourselves justified in seeing it as moving also on a third – that of such experiences of initiation by life itself as Shakespeare himself had in late years undergone.

It is not without significance that Pericles-Apollonius is Prince of Tyre. For in ancient times Tyre had been a significant Mystery Centre.
The Mysteries of the Phoenix – the Mysteries of Death and Resurrection – had their home in Phoenicia, the state of which Tyre was the mother-city. Coins of Ancient Tyre bear a palm-tree, whose Latin name, *Phoenix dacty-lifera*, reminds us that it was in this tree that the phoenix built its nest of spice and burnt itself into new life. The tree is itself a picture of death and resurrection – burn an old palm-tree down to the very roots, and a young one springs up amid the ashes; its new shoots, said to be put forth each month, are thrown up from the centre, while the old outer ones die back and add themselves to the tree-bark; thus there is always death below and new green life above, so that even its outward appearance speaks of resurrection.We shall see how Pericles uses this in his armorial device.

We saw in Chapter I how the birth of Jacchos-Dionysus
in the Mystery Drama of Eleusis prefigured the birth of
Christ on earth, and how, in Æschylos' *Prometheus Bound*,
Herakles as deliverer similarly pointed forward to Christ.
The Mysteries of the Phoenix were also in a very special
way a preparation for Christ's coming to earth, for in the
Mystery Temple of Herakles at Tyre there had been laid
up from early times the greatest treasure in the world –
that emerald dish which shone by night and which was
later called the Grail.

The Queen of Sheba brought this treasure to King
Solomon as a gift from King Hiram of Tyre; that is to
say, Tyre sacrificed for the sake of the mission of the
Jews that experience in its Mysteries which was bodied
forth in the emerald shining by night. When Hiram and
his workmen went from Tyre to build King Solomon's
Temple at Jerusalem, virtue went forth from the Tyrian
Mysteries to assist in the preparation for the building of
the body in which the Cosmic World was to become
flesh. This was another clothing of the same esoteric
truth.

With the withdrawal of this treasure, the Tyrian Mysteries lost their content, so that when Pericles, as prince of
his city-state, is ripe for initiation into its Mysteries, these
Mysteries are already decadent, their holy places taken
over by Baal and Astarte.

So he sets out to seek initiation elsewhere.

First he goes to Antioch, where King Antiochus has a
beautiful daughter, a

> *fair Hesperides,*
> *With golden fruit, but dangerous to be touched.*
>   (I, i)

To win her, a riddle must be guessed; if the prince fails
to guess it, his life is forfeit.
Pericles is given the riddle to read:

> *I am no viper, yet I feed*
> *On mother's flesh that did me breed;*
> *I sought a husband, in which labour*
> *I found that kindness in a father.*
> *He's father, son and husband mild,*
> *I mother, wife, and yet his child.*
> *How they may be, and yet in two,*
> *As you will live, resolve it you.*
>
> *(I, i)*

Pericles, asked to propound the riddle, gasps:

> *All love the womb that their first being bred.*
> *Then give my tongue like leave to love my head.*
>
> *(I, i)*

For the riddle has revealed to Pericles that King Antiochus and his daughter have an incestuous relationship.
The whole picture is one of atavism, of forces which have
outlived their time and so become evil. Those unions
within the close blood-tie which in very ancient times had
fostered the clairvoyant insight of kingship, so that in
Egypt, for example, the Pharaoh and his royal sister were
often joined in lawful wedlock to this end, now produced
only decadent occult forces. Later (II, iv), the Princess
of Antioch is in fact described as a glorious casket filled
with pollution.
Further, even had the princess been pure, she could never

have been that higher self with whom Pericles seeks to
unite; she is not sufficiently individualised even to have
a name – she is merely The Daughter of Antiochus. He
has fallen in love with her merely from the fame of her
beauty; his wooing of her has arisen out of an old pre-
personal type of love, no longer valid.
Where he was formerly attracted, Pericles is now re-
pulsed. He fears, too, that his life will be in danger when
King Antiochus realizes that his secret is known. He
therefore flees home to Tyre.
Here a deep melancholy descends on him. Is he perhaps
inwardly aware that he was drawn to the decadence of
Antioch by a strain of Tyrian decadence in himself?
Realizing that if King Antiochus strikes in vengeance his
innocent city will suffer, he leaves the realm, committing
it to the care of his faithful friend, Helicanus.
Pericles' flight takes the form of an errand of mercy; he
arrives at Tarsus with an argosy of corn for the relief of
that city's famine. Cleon, its Governor, and his wife
Dionyza kneel before him in gratitude, but Pericles insists:

> *We do not look for reverence, but for love.*
> *(I, iv)*

Cleon responds with a vow which casts its shadow forward on the future action of the play:

> *The which when any shall not gratify,*
> *Or pay you with unthankfulness in thought,*
> *Be it our wives, our children or ourselves,*
> *The curse of heaven and men succeed their evils!*
> *(I, iv)*

Where the myth-making faculty is at work, a famine in a land or city points to a soul-lack in its rulers. Later we shall see how the proud, hardened sense-nature of Dionyza leads to an ingratitude which for Shakespeare may well have echoed that which had laid a burden on his own being.

Pericles now receives news from Helicanus that King Antiochus has sent an assassin to Tyre in pursuit of him,

And that in Tarsus was not best
Longer for him to make his rest.

(II, Chorus)

So again he sets sail, and is shipwrecked in the first of his tempests.

In his experience at Antioch, Pericles has come face to face with things in himself in need of transmutation. At the same time, his withdrawing of danger from Tyre with his own person has shown him to have a responsible social conscience; and compassion was active in his relief of the famine at Tarsus. Now begin those outer trials and tribulations which picture forth steps in his inner catharsis; and in these early stages of his soul-history every such step is accompanied by a tempest, for he has not yet achieved the virtues of calmness and equanimity, and his lack of them is reflected in outer Nature.

Pericles, shipwrecked, is cast ashore at Pentapolis. (The stage direction runs: "An open place by the Sea-side. Enter Pericles, wet.") Stripped of everything except one solitary jewel "which still holds his biding on my arm," his ships all lost at sea, denied his own city's harbourage, he has reached that stage on the way to initiation which in the Mysteries was called "homelessness".

Fishermen find and succour him and tell him where he is:

> 1ST FISHERMAN: *This is called Pentapolis, and our king*
> *the good Simonides.*
> PERICLES: *The good Simonides do you call him?*
> 1ST FISHERMAN: *Ay, sir, and he deserves to be so called*
> *for his peaceable reign and good*
> *government.*
>
> *(II, i)*

Bearing in mind Shakespeare's care over names, we can be sure that his use of Pentapolis was not a chance one. Pentapolis points to the future; the Rosicrucians knew the pentagram as the form drawn in the heavens by the movements of the planet Venus, and for them it was a symbol of man in the second half of earth-evolution, when the earth must come to embody love. The good Simonides is like a rough-hewn precursor of those Knights of the Golden Stone in *The Chymical Wedding* who strive for a right social order, for the transubstantiation of society. Already he has achieved a right social order adjusted to his epoch – a community still of classes but in which each class is happy, and where even the court has an atmosphere of simplicity and homeliness. Simonides himself has the savour of good bread, and reminds us how often the early Rosicrucians were humble and simple men.

At Pentapolis, then, Pericles comes again into the sphere of Venus – not this time the debased and polluted Venus of Antioch, but Aphrodite Urania. With the aid not of Cupid's flower but of Dian's bud, he is to meet the Venus of the sky.

In their net the fishermen draw up Pericles' armour, rusty but precious to him because bequeathed to him by his father – in his castaway state he is helped by noble hereditary forces. For the fishermen tell him that the good Simonides

> *hath a fair daughter, and tomorrow is her birthday;*
> *and there are princes and knights come from all parts*
> *of the world to just and tourney for her love.*
>
> *(*II, i*)*

Pericles decides that he, too, will "tourney for the lady". The jewel biding on his arm will purchase him a charger, and one of the fishermen sacrifices his best gown to make him "a pair of bases" (the pleated kilt from waist to knee worn by a horseman).

Thus accoutred, Pericles rides to the Lists, his device

> *A withered branch that's only green at the top;*
> *The motto,* In hac spe vivo.
>
> *(*II, ii*) –*

so exact a description of *Phoenix dactylifera* that one cannot doubt that Shakespeare was indicating to the judicius that the hope in which Pericles was living was that of regeneration through rebirth.

The good Simonides' perspicacity in refusing to "scan the outward habit by the inward man" is presently proved by the shouts of "The Mean Knight!", applauding Pericles as victor. When asked his name and parentage, he replies, with a new humility, that he is "a gentleman

of Tyre, my name Pericles". But to the Princess Thaisa
he is transparent Pericles; as she crowns him with the
wreath of victory, she sees through his rusty armour to
his inward being – "To me he seems like diamond to
glass." This is no longer the old pre-personal love, but
the new personal love, given by ego to ego.
Yet Thaisa, too, is not completely unflawed. She dares
to take Diana's name in vain, bidding her father instantly
dismiss the other suitors on the ground that

> *One twelve moons more she'll wear Diana's livery,*
> *This by the eye of Cynthia hath she vowed,*
> *And on her virgin honour will not break it.*
>
> *(II, v)*

But her next immediate step is to "wed the stranger
knight".
Pericles and Thaisa live happily with King Simonides
till tidings reach them that King Antiochus and his
daughter are now dead and the Tyrians threaten to
make Helicanus their king against his will if Pericles does
not return. Pericles, with Thaisa, who is great with child,
embark for Tyre, while Pentapolis rings with the nine
days' wonder:

> *Our heir-apparent is a king!*
> *Who dream'd, who thought of such a thing?*
>
> *(III, Chorus)*

And now Thaisa's broken vow brings woeful con-
sequences. A great storm arises, with "surges which wash
both heaven and hell"; at its height, Thaisa falls into

travail, and presently her nurse Lychorida brings to the
ravaged Pericles a "fresh-new sea-farer" –

> *Patience, good sir! Do not assist the storm!*
> *Here's all that is left living of your queen –*
> *A little daughter.*
>
> *(III, i)*

Hard on her heels come the sailors, made inexorable by
their sea-superstition:

> *Sir, your queen must overboard; the sea works high,*
> *the wind is loud, and will not lie till the ship be*
> *cleared of the dead.*

Pericles cries, distracted:

> *A terrible childbed hast thou had, my dear;*
> *No light, no fire: nor have I time*
> *To give thee hallow'd to thy grave, but straight*
> *Must cast thee, scarcely coffin'd, in the ooze*
>
> *(III, i)*

He lays Thaisa in a chest, "caulk'd and bitumed ready",
wraps her in "cloth of state", adds spices and jewels and
a letter begging burial for her from any who may find
her. But even before the chest is committed to the surging
waves, the desperate condition of the newborn child
clamours for his attention:

PERICLES: *Thou has as chiding a nativity*
As fire, air, water, earth and heaven can make.
… Mariner, say, what coast is this?
SAILOR: *We are near Tarsus.*
PERICLES: *O, make for Tarsus!*
There I will visit Cleon, for the babe
Cannot hold out to Tyrus. There I'll leave it
At careful nursing.

(III, i)

The chest bearing Thaisa is washed ashore at Ephesus. We see with what artistry and with what esoteric wisdom it has been guided to this destination; for at Ephesus is the Temple of Diana, Thaisa's vow to whom of a year's service has been broken; and at Ephesus are the Mysteries of the Uncreated Word; and from Ephesus are to come St. John's Gospel of the Word made flesh and, later, the western Grail-Stream. Surely here, if anywhere in the world, is the one pre-Christian stream which can bring healing to the Mysteries of Tyre, bereft of their own Grail.

The chest, unopened, is brought into the house of Cerimon, the holiest and the wisest of Shakespeare's wise old men. One senses his spiritual stature in the way he stands before us like a pre-Christian fore-runnner of St. John, using the Ephesus-forces lovingly and healingly to help humanity. He is one from whom virtue can ray forth and work miracles.

We have been told already that he is able to call to his aid

the blest infusions
That dwell in vegetives, in metals, stones …
… and hundreds call themselves

Your creatures, who by you have been restored.
(III, ii)

And now, when he opens the chest, and sees Thaisa lying
there amid spices and treasure, and reads Pericles' inarticulate message –

I, King Pericles, have lost
This queen worth all our mundane cost.
Who finds her, give her burying,
She was the daughter of a king –

his first thought is one of compassion for Pericles:

If thou liv'st, Pericles, thou has a heart
That even cracks for woe.

But his second, hard on its heels, is of Thaisa, and not for
burying, but of raising up:

This chanced tonight.
For look, how fresh she looks. Make fire within!
Fetch hither all the boxes in my closet.
Death may usurp on nature many hours,
And yet the fire of life kindle again
The overpress'd spirits … The fire, the cloths!
The rough and woeful music that we have,
Cause it to sound! The music there!
I pray you, give her air. Gentlemen,

This queen will live; nature awakes, a warmth
Breathes out of her; she hath not been entranc'd
Above five hours. See how she 'gins to blow
Into life's flower again.

(II, ii)

Shakespeare gives no stage directions to accompany
Cerimon's speech. But Gower, in Shakespeare's source,
tells us rather touchingly:

"And with the craftes that he couthe
He sought and found a signe of life.
With that this worthy Kinges wife
Honestely they token out
And maden fires all about.
They laid her on a couche softe,
And with a shete warmed ofte
Her cold brest began to hete,
Her hert also to flacke and bete.
This maister hath her every jointe
With certain oil and balme anointe,
And put a liquor in her mouthe,
Which is to few clerkes couthe,
So that she covereth ate laste."

We feel in Shakespeare's version that we are present at
an intimation of an initiation. The chest in which Thaisa
lies entranced for five hours is reminiscent of the coffin
in which the neophyte lay for three and a half days; the
gentlemen in Cerimon's house had indeed remarked,
"'Tis like a coffin, sir." Like the neophyte, Thaisa has
been raised from a suspension of life which is not yet

death; Cerimon stands beside her like the hierophant, the guardian of and inductor into hidden spiritual knowledge. Through music he is able to command her inner rhythms that the breath of life flows back into her body; the heated cloths wrap her about with fire's healing till the chilled heart beats again.

She had been laid in a chest with spices. ("It smells most sweetly," had been Cerimon's first comment.) Fire had been needed to bring her back to life. Her return follows the pointing of the Phoenix along the same path of mystical death and resurrection.

This is the first of Shakespeare's resurrections.

That she has indeed passed through a catharsis is clear in her first words:

> *O dear Diana!*
> *Where am I? Where's my lord? What world is this?*
> *(III, ii)*

That she honours her earlier vow and now enters Diana's temple as a "votaress" follows naturally.

Pericles, having left his young daughter Marina at Tarsus, in the foster care of Cleon and Dionyza, returns to Tyre:

> PERICLES: *So I take my leave.*
> *Good madam, make me blessed in your care*
> *In bringing up my child.*
> DIONYZA: *I have one myself,*
> *Who shall not be more dear to my respect*
> *Than yours, my lord.*
> *(III, iii)*

But Dionyza's promise takes no cognizance of her own
feminine nature. As Marina grows into graceful maiden-
hood, she eclipses her foster-sister Philoten in everything;
in music and letters she has become "the heart of general
wonder". Dionyza can bear it no longer. She sends her
servant, Leonine, to the seashore, where Marina is scat-
tering flowers on her nurse Lychorida's grave, to murder
her. Like the other persecuted stepchildren of countless
fairy-tales, Marina escapes the murderer's knife; but the
pirates who rescue her take her to Mitylene, where they
sell her into a brothel.

Hitherto she has proved a paragon of scholars; here she
proves unteachable.

> MARINA: *If fires be hot, knives sharp, or waters deep.*
> *Untied I still my virgin knot will keep.*
> *Diana, aid my purpose!*
> BAWD: *What have we to do with Diana?*
>
> *(IV, ii)*

Moreover, she converts the customers to virtue:

> 1ST GENT: *Did you ever hear the like?*
> 2ND GENT: *No, nor never shall in such a place,*
> *she being once gone.*
> 1ST GENT: *But to have divinity preached there! Did you*
> *ever dream of such a thing?*
> 2ND GENT: *No, no. Come, I am for no more*
> *bawdy-houses.*
> *Shall's go hear the vestals sing?*
> 1ST GENT: *I'll do anything now that is virtuous.*
>
> *(IV, v)*

She even converts Lysimachus, the Governor of the city:

> BAWD: *How now, what's the matter?*
> BOULT: *Worse and worse, mistress; she has now spoken*
> *holy words to the Lord Lysimachus.*
> BAWD: *O, abominable!*
> BOULT: *The nobleman would have dealt with her*
> *like a nobleman, and she sent him away as*
> *cold as a snowball: saying his prayers, too.*
>
> *(*IV, vi*)*

In contrast to the destruction of evil in *King Lear*, what Shakespeare is tentatively indicating here is that Manicheism of the future, that redemption of evil by and into good, towards which the old Rosicrucians strove under the image of the transmutation of coal into diamond. Marina is an exact prototype of the Manichean method of dealing with evil, which is not to destroy it, but to allow good to be immersed in it, so that the light of the latter may illuminate and transform the former from within, always subject to its freewill. This is, indeed, what Christ Himself did in descending into matter.

Marina meets evil not by destruction but by creation. In place of the services required of her, she offers all the riches of her culture to the Bawd:

> *If that thy master would gain by me,*
> *Proclaim that I can sing, weave, sew and dance,*
> *And I will undertake all these to teach.*
> *I doubt not that this populous city will*
> *Yield many scholars.*
>
> *(*IV, vi*)*

Gower as Chorus reports her phenomenal success; she becomes as famous a wonder in Mitylene as she had been in Tarsus.

And now the time has come for Pericles to fetch his daughter home. He goes rejoicing to Tarsus, only to be told by Dionyza the false news of Marina's death and to be shown her tomb, with her epitaph written on it in golden letters. Pericles, "in sorrow all devour'd," swears never to cut his hair, puts on sackcloth, and sails away. This time he meets no storm, Gower reports:

> He bears
> A tempest, which his mortal vessel tears,
> And yet he rides it out.
>
> (IV, Chorus)

A strange sickness comes now upon Pericles, a kind of death-in-life which one receives the impression is the result of his having entered on an inner development which he has been unable to bring to fulfilment. He had been momentarily united with Thaisa, his higher self, only to lose her. That gift from the spiritual worlds, their child, he had held momentarily, only to lose her, also. In vowing not to cut his hair, he now attempts to strengthen his links with the spiritual worlds by old methods, no longer lawful. Samson, when those links were cut, had been at Delilah's mercy; but in Samson's day those links had still been legitimate. In myths and fairytales, scissors are a picture of the ego-forces on the crossed focus of human sight; only man has this. In remaining "un-sissor'd," Pericles sinks into lethargy, is reduced to a lower level of consciousness, within too weak an ego-organisation.

When Pericles' ship lies off Mitylene for Neptune's festival, and Lysimachus the Governor comes out on his barge to pay his respects, Helicanus tells him:

> *Sir, our vessel is of Tyre, in it the King,*
> *A man who for three months hath not spoken*
> *To anyone, nor taken sustenance*
> *But to prorogue his grief.*
>
> *(V, i)*

Lysimachus suggests that the wonder-maid of Mitylene be sent for to use her "sacred physic" in an attempt to cure the king; but at first there is no visible reaction

> (Marina sings)
> LYSIMACHUS: *Marked he your music?*
> MARINA: *No, nor looked on us.*
>
> *(V, i)*

Yet something as yet invisible has happened. Man, as the Rosicrucians knew, was first formed by the power of the Word out of the forces of harmony; these are united in Marina's singing, and already their healing flows into the inner void within the being of Pericles. As the scene unfolds, it becomes clear that she has awakened him out of his dumbness and lifted him from a lower state of consciousness into a higher one.

And now she boldly lays hold on his aroused attention:

> *I am a maid,*
> *My lord, which ne'er before invited eyes,*
> *But have been gazed on like a comet.*
>
> *(V, i)*

She is baring her innermost being to him. For – and this again was Rosicrucian knowledge – comets have a spiritual function: to sweep clear the solar system of accumulated evil. Shakespeare reveals knowledge of this when he makes Bedford call on comets to

> *Brandish your crystal tresses in the sky,*
> *And with them scourge the bad revolting stars.*

To one on a path of inner development Marina could not have proclaimed more clearly her Manichean role and why here destiny had led her to a Mitylene brothel.
Now step by step, she unfolds her story to him, on the sound psychological basis that the best medicine of a melancholic is to hear of a fate worse than his own:

> *She speaks,*
> *My lord, that, maybe hath endured a grief*
> *Nigh equal yours, if both were justly weighed.*

At this, Pericles looks at her, and is struck by a resemblance:

> PERICLES: *You are like something that – what*
> *countrywoman?*
> *Here of these shores?*

MARINA: *No, nor of any shores.*
Yet I was mortally brought forth, and am
No other than I appear.
PERICLES: *My dearest wife was like this maid, and*
such a one
My daughter might have been.

Step by step, Marina brings him nearer to discovery:

My name is Marina, for I was born at sea…
My father was a king…
My mother was the daughter of a king,
Who died the minute I was born…
The king my father did in Tarsus leave me
Till cruel Cleon, with his wicked wife,
Did seek to murder me.
A crew of pirates came and rescued me,
Brought me to Mitylene…
I am the daughter to King Pericles…
Thaisa was my mother.

And now Pericles, drawn back step by step to life, weeping (which draws the ego back into the body), opens his heart and arms:

O come hither,
Thou that begett'st him that did thee beget!
(V, i)

Marina, with her "sacred physic," is "another life to

Pericles, thy father." In her is restored something higher in himself which he had lost. She has brought him another step forward on his way of inner development, to the stage known as Inspiration, when the soul becomes able to hear the harmonies of the heavenly worlds. And this is, in fact, precisely what Pericles does now:

PERICLES: *But, what music?*
HELICANUS: *My lord, I hear none.*
PERICLES: *None?*
The music of the spheres! List, my Marina!
Rarest sounds! Most heavenly music!
It nips me unto listening, and thick slumber
Hangs upon mine eyes; let me rest. (Sleeps.
(V, i)

Marina, by her singing, has already begun the restoration of the lost Word, has already pointed delicately to Ephesus. And now, as Pericles sleeps full of divine benisons, having become aware of the cosmic harmonies sounding within himself, Diana herself appears to him, "as in a vision," and directs him to sail to Ephesus and tell his story in her Temple there.

Gower tells us that "in feathered briefness sails are filled". This time there is no tempest; the sea bears the ships smoothly and swiftly to Ephesus; and there, in Diana's Temple, Pericles does as Diana had bidden him.

The High Priestess recognizes him:

O my lord,
Are you not Pericles? Like him you speak,

> *Like him your are. Did you not name a tempest,*
> *A birth, and death?*
>
> *(V, iii)*

Cerimon describes Thaisa's coming to Ephesus, and Pericles sighs out his heart on a breath of joy:

> *This, this! No more, you gods! Your present kindness*
> *Makes my past miseries sport!*
>
> *(V, iii)*

As Marina cries, "My heart leaps to be gone into my mother's bosom," and Pericles draws her into the circle with "Thy burden of the sea," and Thaisa lovingly embraces her with "Blessed and mine own," one has the impression that this is the moment in which Pericles' inner development comes to its fulfilment – an impression confirmed when Pericles gaily announces that "this ornament" (his beard) shall be clipped to grace Marina's marriage to Lysimachus. This will take place at Pentapolis, where, the good Simonides having just died, Pericles and Thaisa will succeed him, while Lysimachus and Marina become King and Queen of Tyre.

So the initiation Pericles had wrongly sought in Antioch he finds at last in Ephesus. It is more, one feels, than a rebirth for himself; it is also a Phoenix-birth for the Mysteries of Tyre. That Marina is to be married at Pentapolis, that earthly reflection of the gestures of the Venus of the sky, bodes well. That she is to reign at Tyre bodes even better. For already, before Grail maidens were, she brings back the Grail to Tyre. What she and Pericles consummate together is a kind of pre-Christian annunciation of the act of healing recorded by St. Luke, when, in healing the daughter of the Syrio-Phoenician woman, Christ Himself also healed the Tyrian Mysteries.

In *Pericles* the creative impulse in Shakespeare has been invaded by the forces of resurrection, and its Marina is the first of a quite new generation of young human beings. In *Cymbeline*, its successor, Imogen and her brothers, Guiderius and Aviragus, carry also the imprint of this new generation, and Imogen herself experiences a kind of echo of an initiation-resurrection. In *The Winter's Tale* we shall now see how both those new youth-forces and those forces of resurrection inform the shaping spirit of the play, and how Shakespeare journeys from the Ephesian to the Eleusinian Mysteries.

CHAPTER XII

THE WINTER'S TALE

"The Mystery cults were performed not to
show men something for their outer eye,
but to awaken inner experience in the
whole human being. Mighty destinies
formed the subject of these cults and
Mysteries."

RUDOLF STEINER[32]

THE WINTER'S TALE is the third of
Shakespeare's plays in which jealousy, that
perverted inversion of love, is portrayed in
most deadly earnest; one feels that at some
time it must have been a very real monster
writhing in his own soul to have left him
with so deep and compassionate a penetration of its
tortures and its torturings.
In *Othello* it ended in tragedy, for Othello had that demi-
devil, Iago, at his side:

Will you, I pray you, demand that demi-devil
Why he hath thus ensnar'd my soul and body"
(Othello, V, vi)

In *Cymbeline*, tragedy was finally averted by Imogen's

magnificent forgiveness of Posthumus' jealousy:

> *Why did you throw your wedded lady from you?*
> *Think that you are upon a rock; and now*
> *Throw me again.*   (Embracing him)
> POSTHUMOUS: *Hang there like fruit, my soul,*
>   *Till the tree die!*
>
>   *(Cymbeline, V, v)*

In *The Winter's Tale* Leontes is confronted with
Hermione''s innocence early in the play; it takes all the
succeeding action, and sixteen years of grief and repentance on Leontes' part, to resolve the tangled and far-
reaching consequence of his brief but catastrophic bout
of jealousy.

In Leontes' case there is no Iago, no Lachimo; to everyone except himself and the wavering Antigonus
Hermione's purity is self-evident. The sudden appearance
of this unfounded jealousy, fully-grown and ravening, out
of a clear sky, has long been an enigma and a stumbling-
block to Shakespearean criticism.

But when one remembers that Leontes was King of
Sicilia, the surmise arises that in this may lie the solution
of the enigma.

For from the times of antiquity Sicily has been known as
a region in which powerful forces of the depths stream
up into man from the soil. This is indicated in the Greek
myth in which Zeus imprisoned alive the hostile
hundred-armed giants Briareus, Enceladus and Typhon
beneath Mt. Etna, so that the land shook with their
struggles, and the fire of their breath belched forth from
the volcano. Here, also, dusky Dis, as he carried off
Persephone, clove a chasm direct into the darkness of the

dreaded Underworld. Here, further, lived the Cyclopes, whose giant bodies were the product of ungoverned life-forces, and whose one eye indicated a decadent form of consciousness surviving from a long-distant past.

In the Middle Ages it was known that the Sicilian Calot Bobot was a stronghold of powerful Luciferic passions, and that it was by utilizing Sicily's dark subterranean forces that Klingsor was able to work so devastatingly against the Knights of the Grail. Where the ego is not sufficiently strong and conscious to remain in complete control, a human being can be at the mercy of this upsurge of chaotic instincts and impulses, especially one in whom the feeling-life predominates, as both Leontes' nature and his name indicate it does in him. In such a case, if a King of Sicilia was not a ruler of himself, Sicilia would rule him.

The source of the first three acts of *The Winter's Tale* was the prose romance *Pandosto* by Robert Greene (he who had bestowed early immortality on Shakespeare as an upstart crow). Shakespeare turned Greene's Sicilians into Bohemians, and his Bohemians into Sicilians. Why he should have juggled thus with *Pandosto's* ethnology has puzzled critics; but if he conceived of Leontes' jealousy as bound up with the Sicily-forces, some light is thrown on this. Moreover, the luxuriant fruitfulness of Sicily was ascribed by the Greeks to the influence of Persephone, who had her earthly home there. From Sicily she was riven away, as Perdita is in the play; and as Shakespeare clearly thinks of Perdita in terms of Persephone, it is also essential that Sicily, not Bohemia, should be her birth-place.

Leontes' jealousy emerges full-panoplied when, at his

desire, Hermione persuades King Polixenes of Bohemia, who has been their guest for nine months, to stay with them a week longer:

Too hot, too hot!
To mingle friendship far is mingling bloods.
I have tremor cordis on me
                                                                        (I, ii)

He demands of his courtier, Camillo, that he shall poison Polixenes. Camillo warns Polixenes, who, analysing the situation with admirable lucidity, decides on flight in Camillo's company:

This jealousy
Is for a precious creature; as she's rare
Must it be great; and as his person's mighty
Must it be violent; and as he doth conceive
His is dishonour'd by a man which ever
Profess'd to him, why, his revenges must
In this be made more bitter ... Come, Camillo;
I will respect thee as a father if
Thou bear'st my life off hence.

To Leontes Polixenes' flight is proof that he has "touch'd the queen forbiddingly," and Camillo's that he was "his pandar; there is a plot against my life, my crown." The child due soon to be born to Hermione is a bastard; therefore – "Away with her to prison!"
                                                                        (II, i)

At the same time, "to give rest to the minds of others," he despatches two lords to consult Apollo's oracle at "sacred Delphos".

Paulina, Antigonus' wife and Hermione's staunch friend, takes the latter's little daughter, prematurely born in prison, to lay at Leontes' feet in the hope that "he may soften at the sight … If I prove honey-mouth'd, let my tongue blister." She is already emerging as the conscience of the king – a conscience so full of pricks that at her appearance he roars:

> *Antigonus,*
> *I charged thee that she should not come about me:*
> I knew she would.
>
> *(II, iii)*

Leontes, incensed, orders Antigonus to take the child away and expose her to the elements "in some desart place quite out of our dominions." In that Antigonus is not fully persuaded of the queen's innocence, he condemns himself to death when he undertakes this task; he has not proved himself worthy to have part in the new world which is already upspringing, though still concealed in the old.

At her trial, Hermione bears all Leontes' vituperations with grave and quiet nobility, appealing at last from his to a higher justice:

> *Your honours all,*
> *I do refer me to the oracle.*
> *Apollo be my judge!*
>
> *(III, ii)*

And when the "holy seal" of the oracle is broken, her vindication is complete:

> 'Hermione is chaste; Polixenes blameless;
> Camillo a true subject; Leontes a jealous
> tyrant; his innocent babe truly begotten;
> and the king shall live without an heir if
> that which is lost be not found.'

But Leontes categorically refuses to believe it:

> There is no truth at all i' the oracle.
> The sessions shall proceed; this is mere falsehood.

With a dreadful immediacy news is brought to him that Mamillius, his little son and heir, has died. He is still young enough to live embraced in his mother's feeling-life, and he has languished from the injuries which she herself has borne with such great patience.
But at these tidings she swoons and is carried out; and Leontes' own feelings swing to the other extreme:

> Apollo's angry: and the heavens themselves
> Do strike at my injustice. Apollo, pardon!
> I'll reconcile me to Polixenes,
> New woo my queen, recall the good Camillo ...

But his dreamings are cut short; Paulina returns to report with blistering tongue that Hermione is dead.

How can that which is lost be found? Antigonus has already departed, taking the new-born babe no-one knows whither. Sicilia again stands where she stood when Persephone was abducted; her fruitfulness fails till the vanished child shall return.

Antigonus is, in point of fact, on the sea-coast of Bohemia, with a great storm blowing up. Hermione, in a dream, has directed him to go there – "places enough are in Bohemia" – has announced that her child's name is to be Perdita, and has prophesied that

> *for this ungentle business*
> *Put on thee by my lord, thou'lt ne'er see*
> *Thy wife Paulina more.*
>
> *(III, iii)*

For Antigonus is small-souled; he cannot grow to the stature which those must attain to have a place to fill in the reborn world to which, by his relationship to the large-hearted Paulina, he should rightly belong. So the first period of the play closes with a light satiric scene (such a note is frequently introduced in *The Chymical Wedding* to avoid any trace of sentimentality) which is nevertheless a soul-drama exteriorised on the stage.

Laying down the babe, and with her a bundle and a letter – "thy character" – he murmurs, "Blossom, speed thee well;" and then, says the stage direction, "Exit, pursued by a bear."

The rest, including the wreck of his ship, with which sinks all knowledge of Perdita's whereabouts, is described by the Clown, who is to become Perdita's Bohemian foster-brother:

I have seen two such sights by sea and by land!
Now the ship boring the moon with her mainmast,
and anon swallowed with yest and froth.
How the poor souls roared, and the sea mocked
them; and how the poor gentleman roared,
and the bear mocked him. *I have not winked*
since I saw these sights; the men are not yet
cold under water, nor the bear half dined
on the gentleman: he's at it now.

And his father, the Old Shepherd who is to save Perdita's
life and so bring about the rebirth of Sicilia, closes the
winter's tale and begins the summer one as he takes up
the child, replying:

Now bless thyself: thou mettest with things
dying, I with things new born.

"Time as Chorus" now wafts us across a gulf of sixteen
years to the Old Shepherd's sheep-shearing feast,
presided over by Perdita, the daughter of the house,
"most goddess-like prank'd-up," with Prince Florizel of
Bohemia, in "swain's clothing", in attendance. We learn
that they met when the prince's "good falcon made her
flight across thy father's ground," and that each so
deeply loves the other that, as the Old Shepherd
presently artlessly tells Polixenes, Florizel's disguised and
irate father,

I think there is not half a kiss to choose

> *Who loves the other best.*
>
> *(IV, iii)*

As Perdita comes forward to greet her guests, herself so
fresh and ardent and so rapturously in love, her arms
filled with "the fairest flowers o' the season," the mask
of mortality slips and we see her standing there quite
openly as that rose of shadow whose true rose is Persephone – Persephone, in whose absence Nature mourns
and winter chills the earth, and at whose return all
creation rejoices, and spring and summer reign. She
stands there like a picture of those forces of resurrection
it is her destiny to bring to Sicilia.

Twice already Shakespeare's imagination has hovered
towards this picture. Once was in *Pericles*, when Marina
is strewing flowers on her nurse Lychorida's grave:

> *I will rob Tellus of her weed,*
> *To strew thy green with flowers; the yellows, blues,*
> *The purple violets, and marigolds*
> *Shall as a carpet hang upon thy grave*
> *While summer days do last.*
>
> *(Pericles, IV, i)*

There Leonine comes to her to murder her. Like the
huntsmen sent by wicked stepmothers in fairy tales on
the same errand, Leonine represents those death-
processes in the organism which accompany the awakening of the intellect at puberty. Marina escapes them, for
in her all knowledge is uplifted into art.

The second was in *Cymbeline*, when Aviragus finds Fidele
(his sister Imogen, disguised as a page) in a drugged
sleep, which he mistakes for death:

With fairest flowers
While summer lasts, and I live here, Fidele,
I'll sweeten thy sad grave; thou shalt not lack
The flower that's like thy face, pale primrose, nor
The azur'd harebell, like thy veins, no, nor
The leaf of eglantine, whom not to slander,
Outsweeten'd not thy breath.

(Cymbeline, IV, ii)

Again the impression is that of an overcoming of death, for presently Imogen awakes from what has been a kind of initiation-sleep.

And now, in *The Winter's Tale*, Perdita, radiant earthly reflection of that other lost one, Persephone, calls by name on her true rose's self:

O Proserpina,
For the flowers now that frightened thou let'st fall
From Dis's waggon! daffodils
That come before the swallow dares, and take
The winds of March with beauty; violets dim,
But sweeter than the lids of Juno's eyes
Or Cytherea's breath; pale primroses,
Bold oxlips, lilies of all kinds. O, these I lack
To make you garlands of, and my sweet friend,
To strew him o'er and o'er!

Floriel instantly and gaily picks up the under-current of death:

What, like a corse?

And a third time, most triumphantly, the forces of death
are routed:

> *No, like a bank for love to lie and play on;*
> *Not like a corse; or of, not to be buried,*
> *But quick, and in mine arms.*
>
> *(The Winter's Tale,* IV, iii*)*

But before Perdita-Persephone can rout Sicilia's winter,
there are tests here in Bohemia to be passed.

When, at the sheep-shearing, Florizel presses to become
betrothed to Perdita, Polixenes, beside himself with
anger, throws off his disguise and threatens the Old
Shepherd, Florizel and Perdita in turn:

> *Thou old traitor,*
> *I am sorry that by hanging thee I can*
> *But shorten thy life one week ... For thee, fond boy,*
> *We'll bar thee from succession ... And you, enchantment,*
> *If ever henceforth thou*
> *Should'st hoop his body more with thy embraces,*
> *I will devise a death as cruel to thee*
> *As thou art tender to it.*

Perdita's comment is naive and fearless:

> *I was not much afeard; for once or twice*
> *I was about to speak and tell him plainly*
> *The self-same sun that shines upon his court*
> *Hides not his visage from our cottage.*

Nevertheless she begs her lover, "Of your own state take care."
But even if it means that the blood-tie must be broken, Florizel stands faithful to the claims of love:

> *What I was, I am ... It cannot fail but by*
> *The violation of my faith; and then*
> *Let nature crush the sides o' the earth together*
> *And mar the seeds within! Lift up thy looks:*
> *From my succession wipe me, father; I*
> *Am heir to my affection.*

Meanwhile, in Sicilia, Leontes, after sixteen years of "saint-like sorrow", is being pressed to marry again for the sake of an heir. Paulina scathingly reminds him:

> *Has not the divine Apollo said*
> *The King Leontes shall not have an heir*
> *Till his lost child be found? ...*
> *Yet if my lord will marry, give me the office*
> *To choose you a queen.*
> LEONTES: *My true Paulina,*
> *We shall not marry till thou bidd'st us.*
> PAULINA: *That*
> *Shall be when your first queen's again in breath;*
> *Never till then.*
>
> *(V, i)*

Early in the play, Leontes' young son, Mamillius, had begun to tell a story, which at an exoteric level gives the play its title:

HERMIONE: *Pray you, sit by us and tell's a tale.*
MAMILLIUS: *Merry or sad shall't be?*
HERMIONE: *As merry as you will.*
MAMILLIUS: *A sad tale's best for winter.*
HERMIONE: *Let's have that.*
MAMILLIUS: *There was a man dwelt by a churchyard.*
I will tell it softly,
Yond crickets shall not hear it.
HERMIONE: *Come on then, and give't me in mine ear.*
(II, i)

And that is all we hear of the story from Mamillius. But for sixteen years Leontes had been that man.

And now, out of the blue, Florizel and Perdita, sent by Camillo (to be out of Polixene's sight "till the fury of his highness settle"), come to Leontes; and at the sight of Perdita the ice around his heart begins to melt. His greeting is directed unconsciously to the Persephone in her:

Fair princess – goddess! Welcome hither
As is the spring to the earth!
(V, i)

Hard on their heels comes Camillo himself, with Polixenes, the Clown, and the Old Shepherd; for the latter, unenamoured of the prospect of hanging, had taken to Polixenes Antigonus' letter, Perdita's baby-bundlings, and the jewels and the "fairy gold" found with her.

And now it is

*nothing but bonfires; the oracle is fulfilled; the king's
daughter is found … the king and Camillo look as they
had heard of a world ransomed – There is such
unity in the proofs – the mantle of Queen Hermione,
her jewel about the neck of it; the letter of Antigonus,
which they know to be his character; a handkerchief
and rings of his that Paulina knows … Our king,
ready to leap out of himself for joy of his found
daughter; then cries, 'O thy mother, thy mother'; then
asks Bohemia forgiveness; then thanks the old shepherd,
which stands by like a weather-beaten conduit of many
kings' reigns … The princess, hearing of her mother's
statue, which is in the keeping of Paulina – a piece
many years in doing – thither with all greediness of
affection are they gone.*

(V, ii)

In the Mystery-myth of Persephone, Demeter searches
day and night for her beloved child, neglecting her care
of the earth, so that Nature grows unfruitful. Even when
found, Persephone can never again be wholly hers, for
she has eaten of a pomegranate in the Underworld, and
therefore must spend half of every year in its darkness.
While she is there, Demeter and Nature mourn – it is
their winter; when she returns to the light of day they
rejoice – it is their summer.

In *Pandosto* the queen of Sicilia is called Bellaria:
Shakespeare changed her name to Hermione. If one ever
doubted that he wrote *The Winter's Tale* with this
Mystery-myth in mind, such doubt disappears before
the discovery that at Syracuse – in Sicily – Demeter was
worshipped under the name of Hermione.

Harmonia, the daughter of Venus and Mars, was also
known as Hermione. We spoke in Chapter VII of her

wonderful necklace of jewels which represented the
harmony of the spheres. In the description of the mantle
in which the new-born Perdita was wrapped – "the
mantle of Queen Hermione, her jewel about the neck of
it" – there seems to be a hint to the judicious: when this
earthly Hermione lost her child, all well-being, all order
in the universe, went with her.

Meeting Leontes again after those sixteen years of saint-
like sorrow, we are aware of a change in him – he has
passed through a catharsis and his soul is now ripe for
rebirth. Looking back at Hermione as we last saw her at
her trial, we remember her as grown grave and immobile,
sapped of vitality and joy. In Demeter, bereft of Persephone, the life-forces were frozen with grief, so that she
and Nature, living, tasted of death. Had Hermione still
been living, this is how we would expect to find her now.
And this, in fact, is how we do find her in Paulina's statue.

In *The Chymical Wedding*, when the wedding-guests work
with alchemical processes to create new bodies for the
young King and Queen, these seem at first to have life
but not yet consciousness, nor do they move or speak.
The Virgin Alchimia and the Warden of the Tower
awaken their consciousness by ritual gestures. They move
through the magic of music. When a prayer has been
offered they speak. Step by same step, Paulina restores
Hermione to her wondering family.

In a deeply moving scene in her chapel, she draws a
curtain and reveals a perfect life-sized statue. All see it
with awe and joy. One is reminded of Themistius'
description of how, after the period of catharsis, "the
priest threw open the propylae of the Temple of Eleusis,
whereupon the statue of the goddess (Demeter) appeared
in full splendour under a burst of light, and the gloom
and darkness of the spectators were dispelled."

LEONTES: *Would you not deem it breath'd?*

PAULINA: *If you can behold,*
I'll make the statue move indeed, descend
And take you by the hand.

LEONTES: *What you can make her do*
I am content to look on; what to speak
I am content to hear.

PAULINA: *Music, awake her! Strike.*   (Music)
'Tis time; descend; be stone no more;
            approach.
Come, I'll fill your grave up; come away;
Bequeath to death your numbness, for from him
Dear life redeems you. You perceive she stirs.
     (Hermione comes down.

LEONTES (embracing her): *O, she's warm!*
If this be magic, let it be an art
Lawful as eating.

PAULINA: *She lives,*
Though yet she speak not. Mark a little while.
Please you to interpose, fair madam: kneel
And pray your mother's blessing. Turn,
        good lady:
Our Perdita is found.
   (Presenting Perdita, who kneels to
    Hermione

HERMIONE: *You gods, look down*
And from your sacred vials pour your graces
Upon my daughter's head! Tell me, mine own,
Where hast thou been preserved? For thou
       shalt hear that I,
Knowing from Paulina that the oracle
Gave hope thou wast in being, have
       preserved myself
To see the issue.

PAULINA: *Go together, you precious winners all …*
(V, iii)

"I'll fill your grave up" were words spoken by the hierophant at the close of an initiation, when the soul returned to the seemingly lifeless body. Paulina, indeed, throughout the scene, acts as hierophant; but it is from Perdita that the new life-forces stream.

The statue scene is not to be regarded as a deception, but as a Mystery-representation. The statue of Hermione is a picture of the winter of the soul awaiting its spring. If we enter fully into her awakening we also feel, as the group in the chapel must have felt, something of the strong workings of catharsis. More, perhaps, than anything else in Shakespeare does it bring home to us that "the function of the Mystery-drama was to awaken inner experience in the whole human being."

At Eleusis the Mystery-Drama of Persephone was performed in February of each year, during the Lesser Mysteries, its aim being to bring about a catharsis preparing the mystae for initiation in the Greater Mysteries, the Mysteries of Dionysos, which were held every fifth year in September. In letting these pictures of Demeter and Persephone live in his imagination, Shakespeare, as it were, traced back his own descent right to those Mysteries of Eleusis which gave birth to Western European Drama.

In *Pericles* we have seen Shakespeare concerned with the Ephesian Mysteries, in *The Winter's Tale* with the Lesser Mysteries of Eleusis. Now, in *The Tempest*, we can experience the workings of his imagination as it contrasts medieval and modern paths of esoteric knowledge and finds, at the dawn of the new ego-consciousness, a new pertinence in the great clarion-call of the Greater Mysteries, the Mysteries of Dionysos – "Know thyself!"

CHAPTER XIII

THE TEMPEST

Then I saw every visible substance turn
Into immortal; every cell new-born
Burned with the holy fire of passion.

This world I saw as on her judgement day,
When the war ends, and the sky rolls away,
And all is light, love and eternity.

KATHLEEN RAINE[33]

THERE is a sense in which, in *The Tempest*, Shakespeare's genius is working and weaving not so much in this world as in the world of archetypes behind it. In this sense all the action is really taking place within the sphere of the soul. We are transported by Prospero's magic arts into those realms beyond the Threshold where such soul-dramas are played out.

The play opens with the tempest of the title. It is not a natural tempest; Miranda suspects that Prospero has raised it:

If by your art, my dearest father, you have
Put the wild waters in this roar, allay them.
O! I have suffer'd
With those that I saw suffer: a brave vessel,

[33] PASSION

Who had, no doubt, some noble creatures in her,
Dash'd all to pieces. O! the cry did knock
Against my very heart

(I, ii)

Prospero confirms her suspicion, but assures her that she can believe neither her eyes nor her ears as regards that shipwreck:

> *Wipe thou thine eyes; have comfort.*
> *The direful spectacle of the wreck, which touch'd*
> *The very virtue of compassion in thee,*
> *I have with such provision in mine art*
> *So safely order'd*
> *That not so much perdition as an hair*
> *Betid to any creature in the vessel*
> *Which thou heard'st cry, which thou saw'st sink.*

And later, Ariel confirms this:

> *Not a hair perish'd;*
> *On their sustaining garment not a blemish,*
> *But fresher than before …*
> *Safely in harbour is the king's ship;*
> *In a deep nook she's hid.*

We have already seen in *Pericles* how tempest without and tempest within are connected. There, in the storm in which Marina was born, the nurse Lychorida tried to calm the distracted prince:

Patience, good sir! Do not assist the storm!

(Pericles, III, i)

Now, in the tempest which opens *The Tempest*, the Boatswain points the same moral to the panic-stricken courtiers:

You mar our labour: keep your cabins; you do assist the storm.

(The Tempest, I, i)

And the saved but solitary Ferdinand finds that,

> *sitting on a bank,*
> *Weeping again the king my father's wreck,*
> *This music crept by me upon the waters,*
> Allaying both their fury and my passion
> *With its sweet air.*

*(*I, ii*)*

This tempest without is the projection of a tempest within Prospero, which in turn is the projection of a tempest without of twelve years earlier:

> *Twelve years since, Miranda, twelve years since,*
> *Thy father was the Duke of Milan and*
> *A prince of power.*
> *My brother and thy uncle, call'd Antonio,*
> *Whom, next thyself of all the world I loved,*
> *To him I put the manage of my state,*
> *Being rapt in secret studies, dedicated*

To closeness and the bettering of my mind,
He needs will be absolute Milan;
Confederates with the King of Naples.
Me and thy crying self, i' the dead of darkness,
They bore some leagues to sea, where they prepar'd
A rotten carcass of a boat, not rigg'd,
Nor tackle, sail nor mast; the very rats
Instinctively had quit it: there they hoist us,
To cry to the sea that roared to us.

And now, twelve years later,

By accident most strange, bountiful Fortune,
Now my dear lady, hath mine enemies
Brought to this shore; and by my prescience
I find my zenith doth depend upon
A most auspicious star, whose influence
If now I court not, but omit, my fortunes
Will ever after droop.

Prospero makes it clear that his expulsion from his dukedom had stemmed from his own one-sidedness – "my
library was dukedom large enough" – and that in his
love of study he had neglected the responsibilities of the
external life placed on him by destiny as head of the
state. He expressly states that it was his being so retired
that "in my false brother awak'd an evil nature". And
while he is grateful to the "noble Neapolitan, Gonzalo,"
for smuggling his books into their leaking boat, he still
describes them unrepentantly as "volumes that I prize
above my dukedom".

It was well known in Rosicrucian circles in Shakespeare's day what a danger there was of men splitting into two types in the age then dawning – of the man who followed spiritual pursuits neglecting his earthly responsibilities, and of the man immersed in earthly pursuits neglecting the spirit. Rosicrucianism itself, in fact, attempted to heal this dichotomy by evolving a new path of spiritual development suited to the consciousness of the new age, which could be followed without loss of faithful attention to the demands of man's responsibilities in the outer affairs of the world.

As early as *Love's Labour's Lost*, Shakespeare has already touched on this evasion of responsibility as inherent in the young King of Navarre's suggestion of self-segregation for philosophic study:

> *So study evermore is overshot,*
> *While it would study to have what it would,*
> *It doth forget to do the thing it should.*
>
> *(Love's Labour's Lost, I, i)*

And now, in *The Tempest*, he carries this evasion of responsibility to its logical conclusion – Prospero, as a man of the first type, has precipitated his own and Miranda's plight and has placed Milan and its inhabitants in the power of an unscrupulous example of the second type.

The twelve years of his exile Prospero has perforce applied to the studies to which he has always been drawn, so that he has acquired a high proficiency in those arts which can give a man authority over the elemental beings, and has so attained the powers of a magician.

But this is the first time he has used those powers to inter-
fere in human destiny – it is, indeed, the first time the
possibility has occurred – and thus a quite new moral
problem has presented itself to him.
Twice further in this early scene Prospero mentions a
period of twelve years. Once is when he reminds Ariel
of how he released him from the cloven pine in which
Sycorax, Caliban's mother had confined him –

> *Within which rift*
> *Imprison'd, thou didst painfully remain*
> *A dozen years.*

And again when he threatens Ariel:

> *If thou more murmur'st, I will rend an oak*
> *And peg thee in his knotty entrails till*
> *Thou has howl'd away twelve winters.*

Twelve years is the rhythm of Jupiter – the period in
which this planet makes a complete orbit. It would
therefore seem that the Jupiter-forces are important in
the unfolding of Prospero's life, and even, since it is
twelve years since the last event of great magnitude in
that life occurred, that Jupiter is the "auspicious star"
whose influence it is imperative he should at this moment
court.
A man's consciousness changes in a rhythm of twelve
years. In each such rhythm, said the Rosicrucians, Jupiter
seeks to lead him a step deeper into his own realm, which

is that of wisdom and the shaping of destiny. Twelve
years ago, Prospero's one-sided interest in life led him a
step deeper into that realm of wisdom in a one-sided way.
Now that the rhythm returns, the question is how Prospero will use it and on what level he will grasp the
opportunity it offers to reach his zenith or ever after let
his fortunes droop.

Already in his opening recital of their past history to
Miranda, Prospero has made a gesture of appeal simple
and homely but potentially significant.

> *Lend thy hand,*
> *And pluck my magic garment from me. – So:*
> *Lie there, my art.*   (Lays down his mantle)

It holds a nebulous hint of possibility of this new
influx of Jupiter's wisdom culminating in a sacrifice of
all the power Prospero has spent the past twelve years in
building up. The fact that it is of Miranda that he asks
this help – Miranda, who may be thought of in one
aspect as the still virginal and unfallen forces of his own
soul – suggests that his recent yielding to temptation has
raised in his higher self the question as to whether the
path of magic is after all the true path of inner development for him.

For how has he just used his magical arts? His prescience
of the King of Naples' proximity on his voyage home
after his daughter Claribel's marriage to the King of
Tunis has agitated his twelve-year-old reaction to a
treacherous act into a tempest within, which he has
projected into a tempest without, which has cast up on
his island the perpetrators of that act and has placed

them in his power. It is significant of his inner attitude that he still speaks of them as his enemies – "Bountiful Fortune hath mine enemies brought to this shore."

Prospero stands before us as an enigmatic figure, clearly a soul of great stature, yet in his spiritual development less perfect than, for example, Cerimon in *Pericles*. Profound as his spiritual studies have been along the lines he has chosen there are things in him in need of purification of which he seems yet unaware. He infringes on Miranda's freewill, putting her into a magical sleep to further his own ends; he flares into fury when Ariel pleads for the freedom already promised him; he reviles Caliban. From the fact that later he renounces vengeance on those who twelve years ago had wronged him it is possible to deduce that at present he proposes it.

As a first step in that vengeance, Antonio (his usurping brother) and Alonso and Sebastian (The King of Naples and his brother, both of whom aided and abetted that usurping) are to be brought face to face with their own evil deeds.

But that is the function of Purgatory. Prospero's enchanted island is, in fact, to take over the function of Purgatory.

From external evidence the writing of *The Tempest* would seem to have followed hard on the heels of the writing of *The Winter's Tale*, even probably in the same year (1611); and from internal, after-echoes of his immersion in the Eleusinian Mysteries in one play would seem to have sounded over into his shaping of the other. Among the experiences which, in these Mysteries, led the candidates for initiation through a catharsis were the agonies of an illusory death by drowning; and it is with this experience that *The Tempest* opens, when the shrieks she hears from Prospero's equally illusory shipwreck wring from

Miranda's heart the cry, "O! I have suffer'd with those that I saw suffer." The mystae were led through a realm of darkness, storm and unknown terrors; Plutarch tells of their passing through "a succession of errors of painful wanderings by tortuous ways" – an exact description of Alonso's wanderings on the island in demented search for Ferdinand, his lost son, and of those of Trinculo the jester and Stephano the drunken butler, decoyed by Ariel's invisible music, "played by a picture of Nobody." References abound to the purgatorial cramps, pinches and convulsions with which the island is infested for wrong-doers; and with the snatching away of the banquet laid before them by spirits the distracted castaways live again through the experiences of the harpy-haunted feast of Phineas and of the torments of Tantalus in Hades. Ferdinand's outcry when Ariel leaps about the ship-wreck, "flaming amazement" – "Hell is empty and all the devils are here" (I, ii) – has a certain warranty where the conscience is not clear.

On Prospero's enchanted island, as in the Mysteries, only souls who are sufficiently prepared are purged by pity and terror. Antonio, Prospero's usurping brother, re-mains hardened and unrepentant, and even here, in this place of the torments of purification, he seduces Sebastian into a plot to kill the latter's brother, King Alonso, and seize the throne of Naples:

SEBASTIAN: *I remember*
You did supplant your brother Prospero.
ANTONIO: *True;*
And look how well my garments sit upon me.
SEBASTIAN: *But, for your conscience –*
ANTONIO: *I feel not*

> *This deity in my bosom: twenty consciences,*
> *That stand 'twixt me and Milan, candied*
> *be they,*
> *And melt ere they molest!*

SEBASTIAN: *Thy case, dear friend,*
> *Shall be my precedent: as thou got'st Milan,*
> *I'll come by Naples.*

(II, i)

Ariel, by awakening Gonzalo just as they draw their swords, saves both him and King Alonso from assassination; and later, in his guise as harpy, amid thunder and lightning, he holds up before Alonso, Sebastian and Antonio Purgatory's picture of themselves:

> *You are three men of sin, whom Destiny –*
> *That hath to instrument this lower world*
> *And what is in't – the never-surfeited sea*
> *Hath caused to belch up you; and on this island*
> *Where man doth not inhabit; you 'mongst men*
> *Being most unfit to live.   You three*
> *From Milan did supplant good Prospero;*
> *Expos'd unto the sea, which hath requit it,*
> *Him and his innocent child; for which foul deed*
> *The powers, delaying, not forgetting, have*
> *Incens'd the seas and shores, yea, all the creatures,*
> *Against your peace. Thee of thy son, Alonso,*
> *They have bereft; and do pronounce, by me,*
> *Lingering perdition shall step by step attend*
> *You and your ways; whose wraths to guard you from –*
> *Which here, in this most desolate isle, else falls*
> *Upon your heads – is nothing but heart-sorrow*
> *And a clear life ensuing.*

(III, iii)

Gonzalo notes the workings of this strong indictment in the three men of sin:

All three of them are desperate; their great guilt,
Like poison given to work a great time after,
Now 'gins to bite the spirits.

In Antonio and Sebastian this desperation takes the form of defiance: "One fiend at a time, I'll fight their legions o'er – I'll be thy second." But in King Alonso Ariel's words have rudely shaken his conscience awake, and now he cannot escape its hounding. His own loss of his son Ferdinand, which had filled his whole horizon to the exclusion of all other thought or feeling, he sees now as a punishment for his former perfidy to Prospero:

O, it is monstrous! monstrous!
Methough the billows spoke and told me of it;
The winds did sing it to me; and the thunder,
That deep and dreadful organ-pipe, pronounc'd
The name of Prosper: it did bass my trespass.
Therefore my son i' th' ooze is bedded; and
I'll seek him deeper than e'er plummet sounded,
And with him there lie mudded.

What Alonso believes of Ferdinand – that i' th' ooze lies bedded – Ferdinand, his fears confirmed by Ariel's "Full fathom five thy father lies," also believes of Alonso. Ariel's song would seem superficially to be an intimation that King Alonso has been drowned. But taken on another level it has another meaning. "He hath suffered a sea-change into something rich and strange" lays the foundation beforehand for that transformation of soul which we do indeed now find actually beginning to take place – heart-sorrow and a clear life ensuing. In the Mysteries of Dionysos this first stage of purification was symbolised by immersion in the sea; on the first of their nine days, the call rang out and was obeyed: "Seaward, O mystae!"

Prospero, as from above he watches Ariel hold up the mirror before the three men of sin, would seem still to be thinking and planning in terms of Old Testament justice:

> *My high charms work,*
> *And these mine enemies are all knit up*
> *In their distractions:* they now are in my power.

Meanwhile the nobler part of his plan – the union of Ferdinand with Miranda – unfolds auspiciously.
It has been clear that he was planning this from when he brought about their first meeting:

PROSPERO: *The fringed curtains of thine eyes advance,*
And say what thou seest yond.
MIRANDA: *What is't. A spirit? Believe me, sir,*
It carries a brave form. I might call him
A thing divine; for nothing natural
I ever saw so noble.
PROSPERO (Aside): *It goes on, I see, as my soul*
prompts …

FERDINAND: *Might I but through my prison once a day*
Behold this maid, all corners else o' th' earth
Let liberty make use of.
PROSPERO (Aside): *It works.*

(I, ii)

Step by step the two young souls, the one noble in innocence, the other noble in experience, draw nearer to each other; and always Prospero rejoices:

FERDINAND: *The mistress whom I serve quickens what's*
dead
And makes my labours pleasures. You, O you,
So perfect and so peerless, were created
Of every creature's best.
The very instant I saw you did
My heart fly to thy service.
PROSPERO (Aside): *Fair encounter*
Of two most rare affections! Heavens rain
grace
On that which breed between them! …
MIRANDA: *I am your wife if you will marry me.*
FERDINAND: *Ay, with a heart as willing*
As bondage e' er of freedom.
PROSPERO (Aside): *My rejoicing*
At nothing could be more.

(III, i)

As in all marriages which have a mystical aspect, tests have been set; and now, coming from Ariel's scene with the three men of sin, Prospero announces to the young couple that Ferdinand has passed them all and that they may be betrothed:

If I have too austerely punish'd you,
Your compensation makes amends.
                    All my vexations
Were but my trials of thy love, and thou
Hast strangely stood the test: here, afore Heaven,
As my rich gift and thine own acquisition,
Worthily purchas'd, take my daughter.
                                          (IV, i)

Prospero has promised to "bestow upon the eyes of this young couple some vanity of mine art". So now, after soft music, Ariel presents a Masque; and again through this echo the Eleusinian Mysteries.

Iris, the "many-colour'd messenger" between heaven and earth, is sent by Juno, the goddess of marriage, to summon her "bounteous sister", Ceres (Demeter), the goddess of Nature,

A contract of true love to celebrate,
And some donation freely to estate
On the bless'd lovers.

Ceres enquires anxiously as to whether Venus and Eros will be there.

Since they did plot
The means that dusky Dis my daughter got,
Her and her blind boy's scandal'd company
I have foresworn.

Iris assures her they will not be present:

> *Here thought they to have done*
> *Some wanton charm upon this man and maid,*
> *Whose vows are, that no bed-rite shall be paid*
> *Till Hymen's torch be lighted; but in vain.*

Juno, approaching, begs of Ceres:

> *Go with me*
> *To bless this twain, that they may prosperous be,*
> *And honoured in their issue.*

Juno sings a marriage-blessing over them, and Ceres promises:

> *Spring come to you at the farthest*
> *In the very end of harvest.*

Prospero is placing before "young Ferdinand and his and my lov'd darling" the archetypal picture of their own marriage – a uniting of Juno's chastity with Ceres' fruitfulness, blessed by both heaven and earth.

Ferdinand is deeply moved:

> *This is a most majestic vision.*
> *Let me live here ever:*
> *So rare a wonder'd father and a wise*
> *Makes this place Paradise.*

Iris now calls "temperate nymphs and sunburn'd sicklemen" to "help to celebrate a contract of true love" with "a grateful dance, towards the end whereof Prospero starts suddenly".

> *Alas, I had forgot that foul conspiracy*
> *Of the beast Caliban and his confederates*
> *Against my life: the minute of their plot*
> *Is almost come.*

His perturbation is not only made in itself very evident, but is made more so by the deep concern of the two lovers:

> FERDINAND: *This is strange: your father's in some passion*
> *That works him strongly.*
> MIRANDA: *Never till this day*
> *Saw I him touch'd with anger so distemper'd.*

Yet one cannot think that he is seriously disturbed by the threat to his life *as such*; with his magical arts, that can be easily countered – and indeed is.
His request to Ferdinand not to be concerned runs straight on into (of all things) the famous lines about the cloud-capp'd towers:

> *You do look, my son, in a mov'd sort,*
> *As if you were dismay'd: be cheerful, sir:*
> *Our revels now are ended. These our actors,*
> *As I foretold you, were all spirits and*

Are melted into air, into thin air:
And, like the baseless fabric of this vision,
The cloud-capp'd towers, the gorgeous palaces,
The solemn temples, the great globe itself,
Yea, all which it inherit, shall dissolve
And, like this insubstantial pageant faded,
Leave not a wrack behind. We are such stuff
As dreams are made of, and our little life
Is rounded with a sleep.

In the Masque the actors were spirits; the parts they played, visible, substantial, were semblances, rose's shadows. The spirits have retired from their visible, substantial unreality in the Masque to their invisible unsubstantial reality in the realm of the true rose. The great globe itself is only a reflected reality, of which the archetypal reality is in Plato's World of Ideas. Prospero reveals the secret of matter as the Rosicrucians knew it – which was that all material substance is the external manifestation of the *prima materia* that lies behind it, that all created phenomena are born out of primal Ideas. During our waking life, when we live immersed in the rose's shadow and take it for the true rose, we too are but roses' shadows. Only when man leaves his physical body in sleep and enters the realm of the true rose is he truly awake; in his daytime consciousness he "dreams" matter. Thus in Prospero's words rings an echo of Sophocles'

"I see we're nothing else, just as we are,
But dreams; our life is but a fleeting shadow."

Saying all this does not still Prospero's agitation; rather

it seems to exacerbate it, for he continues immediately:

> *Sir, I am vex'd:*
> *Bear with my weakness; my old brain is troubled.*
> *Be not disturb'd with my infirmity.*
> *If you be pleas'd, retire into my cell*
> *And there repose: a turn or two I'll walk,*
> *To still my beating mind.*
> FERDINAND, MIRANDA: *We wish you peace.*

As soon as Prospero is alone, and has bidden Ariel set out glittering gauds to deflect the would-be murderers from their purpose, his thoughts dwell on Caliban:

> *A devil, a born devil, on whose nature*
> *Nurture can never stick; on whom my pains,*
> *Humanely taken, are all lost, quite lost.*

Later he is to say to King Alonso, of the three would-be murderers:

> *Two of these fellows you*
> *Must know and own;* this thing of darkness I
> Acknowledge mine.
>
> *(V, i)*

He acknowledges Caliban as part of himself as, in *King Lear*, Lear acknowledges Goneril:

But yet thou art my flesh, my blood, my daughter,
Or rather a disease that's in my flesh,
Which I must needs call mine: thou art a boil
In my corrupted blood.

(King Lear, II, iv)

Is one perhaps justified in the surmise that what has so deeply undermined Prospero's equanimity is the realization that Caliban, the still unredeemed forces in himself, is, in spite of all his attempts to transform him, a threat to his own higher nature? The last words spoken before this inner tempest shook him had been Ferdinand's "So rare a wonder'd father and a wise." Had that word *wise* perhaps stabbed him into awareness? *Wonder'd*, yes, with all his magical accomplishments; but had the path of wisdom he had followed been the highest open to him? The memory of Caliban's earlier threat to that which was best and purest on the island must have added its own warning to that awareness:

PROSPERO: *I have us'd thee,*
             Filth as thou art, with human care; and
                                               lodged thee
             In mine own cell, till thou didst seek to
                                                  violate
             The honour of my child,
CALIBAN: *Oh ho! Oh ho! – Would it had been done!*
             Thou did'st prevent me; I had peopled else
             This isle with Calibans.

(The Tempest, I, ii)

Calibans' mother, that

damn'd witch, Sycorax,
For mischiefs manifold and sorceries terrible
To enter human hearing, from Argier
Was banished.

What, when, would have happened had Caliban succeeded in peopling the isle with Calibans? The Prospero-impulse would have been subjugated to the Sycorax-impulse. White magic would have degenerated into black.

But as long as Prospero followed the path of magic with the least hint of Caliban still left unredeemed in his own nature, the peril was always present of white magic degenerating into black.

Unless the personality was completely purified, pride and egoism lay in wait, and the dreams brought into terrestrial materialisation by even the whitest magic could be false ones. The ancients said that true dreams came forth from celestial realms through gates of horn, false ones through gates of ivory. Had he anywhere failed to be transparent Prospero, to apprehend the true rose clearly through the clear gates of horn? Or had he, through the opaque gates of ivory, brought it down into distorted substantially?

The three men of sin are in process of being brought to know themselves. Suddenly Prospero himself is sharing their experience. He is brought sharply face to face with an exercise in drastic self-knowledge.

Through the wielding of his magical arts he has become for himself a kind of demiurge; and now he becomes aware that he is only a human being after all, and a human being only good in parts. In the picture of Caliban lurking in himself he goes through that Mystery

Threshold-experience known as "meeting the Lesser Guardian". It is at this moment that a transformation begins in Prospero which we can follow step by step.
Till now he has spoken of his enemies as being "in my power". Now he says:

> *At this hour*
> Lie at my mercy *all mine enemies.*
> *(IV, i)*

It is an ambiguous phrase; but its ambiguity holds possibilities which take on firmer outline in the scene which follows:

PROSPERO: *How fares the king and's followers?*
ARIEL: *Brimful of sorrow; your charm so strongly*
works them
That if you now beheld them, your
affections
Would become tender.
PROSPERO: *Dost thou think so, spirit?*
ARIEL: *Mine would sir, were I human.*
PROSPERO: *And mine shall.*
Hast thou, which are but air, a touch, a
feeling
Of their afflictions, and shall not myself,
One of their kind, that relish all as sharply,
Passion as they, be kindlier moved than,
thou art?
Though with their high wrongs I am struck
to the quick,
Yet with my nobler reason 'gainst my fury

Do I take part: the rarer action is
In virtue than in vengeance: they being
                                    penitent,
The sole drift of my purpose doth extend
Not a frown further. Go, release them, Ariel.
My charms I'll break, their senses I'll restore.
And they shall be themselves.

                    (V, i)

Caliban has made Prospero aware of his lower self, Ariel
of the opportunities for generosity offered to this higher
self. It is compassion – that virtue which, together with
wonder, distinguishes Miranda – which moves him to
renounce revenge. We may say that it is the Miranda-
forces in him which bring him to this "rarer action."
But what does it mean that "they shall be themselves?"
The purification of Purgatory consists in confronting the
soul with its own acts. That the three men of sin may be
confronted with theirs, he has conjured up a private
Purgatory on his island. And now he finds himself in that
same Purgatory, confronted by his own.
Mankind had once been guided like children by its
spiritual leaders, in a sense by magical means; but that
was when men *were* children, and the spiritual leaders
were exalted and completely selfless beings. But such
omnipotence was no longer lawful in an age of ego-
consciousness. Now whatever earthly decisions were
made as regards men's destinies men had to be free to
make themselves.
But Prospero, with his magical arts, had diverted his
enemies from the homeward voyage they had planned.
He has imposed his will on theirs. Nor has he done this
selflessly, but to implement his revenge. White magic
had already, by this deed of his lower self, degenerated

into rough magic; and rough magic was already the first step on the downward path to black.

No longer can he infringe on their freewill. No longer can he infringe on any man's. The dignity of man demands that they shall be themselves.

There is therefore only one course open to him: he must sacrifice his power as a magician.

And this he now proceeds to do:

> *Ye elves of hills, brooks, standing lakes and groves,*
> *And ye that on the sands with printless foot*
> *Do chase the ebbing Neptune; by whose aid*
> *I have called forth the mutinous winds,*
> *And 'twixt the green sea and the azur'd vault*
> *Set raging war … this rough magic*
> *I here abjure; and when I have requir'd*
> *Some heavenly music – which even now I do –*
> *To work mine end upon their senses that*
> *This airy charm is for, I'll break my staff,*
> *Bury it certain fathoms in the earth,*
> *And deeper than did ever plummet sound*
> *I'll drown my book.*

It is an amazing act of renunciation, an ego-decision carried out in complete solitude. But why is it to the elves of hills, brooks, standing lakes and groves that he announces it?

If he has wronged men by exerting unlawful authority over their fates, he has equally wronged these elemental beings. His studies have revealed to him the secrets of matter; he knows that it is visible and tangible only because these beings are enchanted into it. He knows that is is man's task to free them from their captivity;

yet he has doubly imprisoned them by coercing them to
his service.

So now, in a culminating act of renunciation, he gives
them all, with Ariel, their freedom.

When Ariel conducts King Alonso and his courtiers into
Prospero's presence, we see that the king's catharsis is
complete. For when he mourns his loss of his "dear son
Ferdinand," and Prospero tells him that he, too, has lost
his daughter, Alonso reveals a new and spontaneous
readiness to sacrifice himself for the future:

> *A daughter?*
> *O heavens! That they were living both in Naples,*
> *The king and queen there! that they were, I wish*
> *Myself were mudded in that oozy bed*
> *Where my son lies.*

Prospero promises him::

> *My dukedom since you have given me again,*
> *I will requite you with as good a thing;*

and the entrance of his cell opens, revealing the lost son
and the lost daughter playing chess – a scene reminiscent
of that in *The Chymical Wedding*, in which "the King and
Queen began to play together a game not unlike chess,
with the virtues and vices one against another, where it
might be observed with what plots the vices lay in wait
for the virtues, and how to re-encounter them" – almost

an epitome of the soul-drama of *The Tempest*.

Gonzalo, who is himself, a being of some inner stature and spiritual discernment, had realized from the first that what met them on the island was no mere external experience –

> *Methinks our garments are now as fresh as*
> *when we put them on first in Afric, at the*
> *marriage of the king's fair daughter Claribel.*
> *(II, i)*

And it is he who, rejoicing now at the sight of Ferdinand and Miranda, discerns the finger of fate in all that has happened:

> *Look down, ye gods,*
> *And on this couple drop a blessed crown;*
> *For it is you who have chalk'd forth the way*
> *Which brought us hither!*
> *Was Milan thrust from Milan, that his issue*
> *Should become kings of Naples? In one voyage*
> *Did Claribel her husband find at Tunis,*
> *And Ferdinand, her brother, found a wife*
> *Where he himself was lost; Prospero his dukedom*
> *In a poor isle; and all of us ourselves,*
> *When no man was his own.*
> *(V, i)*

He sees how higher powers have used Prospero's machinations to further their own higher ends; even his faults and failings have been tools to their hands. Indeed, Gonzalo himself had been an early minister of

that same Fate, in that it was he who had placed in
Prospero's rotten carcass of a boat the books which led to
all that followed his finding of the island.

Prospero promises, "calm seas, auspicious gales" for the
voyage home – tempests stilled both without and within.
To Caliban's nature nurture begins to stick:

> *I'll be wise hereafter,*
> *And seek for grace.*

And even in Stephano a new impulse of his true being
hiccups through his cups, defying Machiavelli:

> *Everyman shift for all the rest, and*
> *let no man take care for himself.*

Prospero arranges with "your highness and your train"
that

> *in the morn*
> *I'll bring you to your ship, and so to Naples,*
> *Where I have hope to see the nuptial*
> *Of these our dear-beloved solemniz'd;*
> *And thence retire me to my Milan, where*
> *Every third thought shall be my grave.*

This is no snatching back of worldly pomp and

circumstance, but an acceptance of those earthly responsibilities he had formerly rejected. In him, we may be assured, spiritual development and discharge of earthly tasks will now march forward hand in hand.

And "every third thought shall be my grave." For beyond the grave the souls must go through purification in real earnest. It must come face to face with all its own earthly deeds; and there it cannot sidestep them with hardened heart and ribald tongue, as Sebastian and Antonio did in the enchanted island, or, like Trinculo and Stephano, pass through these profound experiences in a state of sottish unawareness. In actuality, as the Rosicrucians knew, every night of our lives is a kind of miniature rehearsal of this confronting, in which, in sleep, we review and assess our actions of the past day; and since we pass one third of our life in sleep, there is a sense in which every third thought is already our grave, whether we will it or not.

But the Rosicrucians also practised the Pythagorean custom of conducting this nightly review and assessment consciously before sleeping. In the light of this we can perhaps take Prospero's remark as intimating that henceforth his life will be a threefold activity – one third devoted to the wise ruling of his dukedom, one third to his esoteric studies, and one third to purification through rigorous self-examination.

In the Tower of Olympus in *The Chymical Wedding*, Jupiter is revealed as the planetary architect of the future. Prospero at the high hour of his auspicious star has made costly but right decisions. He has abjured the medieval path of magic in favour of the modern path of self-knowledge and self-cleansing; he has renounced rough magic and even white magic in favour of moral magic.

Now he stands stripped by his own freewill of staff, book and mantle, of all power and authority. He has deliberately gone through a kind of death-experience and has been reborn naked into the world. He is ready to set out afresh on a new spiritual path as the rawest of beginners (though by his deed of sacrifice better equipped in virtue than he himself is aware of). And in a new mood of humility, in his deeply moving Epilogue, he appeals to humanity for the human aid all men can give each other:

Now my charms are all o'erthrown,
And what strength I have's mine own;
Which is most faint. Now I want
Spirits to enforce, art to enchant;
And my ending is despair
Unless I be reliev'd by prayer.
As you from crimes would pardon'd be,
Let your indulgence set me free.

When Pericles comes with his soul's history to the Temple of Ephesus, Thaisa asks of him:

Did you not name a tempest,
A birth, and death?

                                        (Pericles, V, iii)

At the end of *The Tempest* we may ask of Shakespeare:

Did you not name a tempest,
A death, and birth?

CHAPTER XIV

EPILOGUE

"No death is more glorious than that
which brings life.
No life is nobler than that which
spring from death.
God Himself, in willing that thou
shoulds't live, must die."

ANGELUS SILESIUS

S O we can live with, and over into Shakespeare's flowering of the spirit, from root
through shoot and leaf and bud to blossom.
We can share with him successive phases in
the unfolding of life-experience, feeling on
our own pulses how some brought him to a
Phoenix-death and some to a Phoenix-resurrection.
With him we can enter into those quiet moments when
he opens to receive a seed for the future as a child
receives a fairytale, and marvel at the later miracle of
the seed grown into a tree, as the fairytale grows into a
moral impulse.

We have watched the seed of mercy, begged as a boon
by Portia, grow into such a tree in Posthumus and
Prospero – in Posthumus all the more marvellous by
contrast with Boccaccio's punishment of Iachimo's
prototype in Shakespeare's source, where he is smeared

with honey, impaled alive on a stake, and stung to death by wasps and hornets. We have seen how Cordelia – like Parsifal, who could not achieve the Grail until he had experienced the sufferings of Amfortas – ripens into compassion through her suffering with suffering Lear, and how in the later-born Miranda compassion is already a "given" attribute.

We have seen how the conflict in Hamlet between "excitements of my reason and my blood" is later resolved in Prospero into "with my nobler reason 'gainst my fury do I take part;" and how the problem of moderation, the Platonic virtue it is specially laid upon our age to strive for, first lightly touched on in *The Merchant of Venice*, is later explored with an almost clinical ruthlessness in *Timon of Athens*.

On every hand, as his soul's history unfolds, we are aware of a ripening and a deepening in Shakespeare. Like Lorenzo can describe to "pretty Jessica" the music of the spheres, but he had to confess that even in heavenly Belmont,

> *Whilst this muddy vesture of decay*
> *Doth grossly close it in, we cannot hear it.*
> (The Merchant of Venice, V, i)

But Pericles, the man on a path of inner development, can hear it. Hearing it marks, in fact, a stage along that path. Hearing it, he is able to go out into the cosmos in a kind of Temple sleep which brings him healing. Hearing it, he finds the spiritual worlds open and Diana appears to him.

In *Love's Labour's Lost* Shakespeare brings a prentice hand to the tentative portraying of the finding of the Idea behind the phenomenon. In *A Midsummer Night's Dream* he playfully explores this finding in terms of gates of ivory and gates of horn. In the last romances he brings us to the very threshold of the realm from which the original ideals of humanity were brought down – the realm from which came the Mystery-teachings; and in *The Tempest*, the last of these romances, for one majestic moment he looks into this realm with the clear sight of the seer.

In *A Midsummer Night's Dream* it is by the eye's enchanment that Lysander glimpses the Hermia in Helena, and Titania the angel and the gentleman in Bottom. Later, it is with formerly blind eyes washed clear by suffering that Lear apprehends the immortal spirit in cast-off Cordelia. At the end, Miranda's new, pure, penetrating vision needs neither magic flower nor life's schooling to help it to pierce direct to the "piece of Divinity" in man; the moment her gaze encounters the wretches cast up on her father's island, she exclaims in rapture:

> *How beauteous mankind is! O brave new world*
> *That has such people in't!*
>
> (The Tempest, V, i)

In *The Merchant of Venice*, Portia acts as hierophant. Lorenzo speaks of her "godlike amity" (III, iv), and she herself indicates to Bassanio a "worthiness" in her which he has not recognized (V, i). Yet, in spite of all her tests and terrors ("You must prepare your bosom for his knife" – IV, i), we are so dazzled by her human attributes, her wit and charm and tender femininity, that we can easily overlook her high Mystery function of leading not only Shylock but also Antonio and even Bassanio through a catharsis of fear. But when Shakespeare reaches *Pericles*, he himself having grown in spiritual stature, he is able to portray such stature in Cerimon. Even without Thaisa's

> *This man*
> *Through whom the gods have shown their power*
> *(V, iii)*

and Pericles'

> *The gods can have no mortal officer*
> *More like a god than you,*
> *(V, iii)*

we are aware of him as the most hieratical figure in the entire range of Shakespeare's plays.

Permeating all this manifold ripening and deepening, there is a sense of Rosicrucianism, which he had begun by regarding more theoretically, working in Shakespeare with even greater power, until, in *Pericles*, what in the earliest plays had been – though eagerly apprehended with both head and heart – still largely academic, leaps into life, with the shaping and informing force of direct experience, as a first-hand reporting in this world's language of another world's truths.

But first there is that period, following *Hamlet*, when the second stage of Parsifal's Grail-quest – the realization that the fault is in ourselves – is explored in every direction. Shakespeare seems now to be saying with Matthew Arnold:

"In tragic life, God wot,
No villain need be; passion spins the plot;
We are betrayed by what is false within."

The whole stage on which the succeeding group of
tragedies is played becomes an inner one. Heaven's
Tower and Hell's Mouth are at war *within* the chief
protagonists, each of whom has a special Hell's Mouth of
his own – Othello, the viper of jealousy uncoiling,
drawing sustenance from the ruthless evil in Iago;
Macbeth, dependence on a decadent clairvoyance out of
time and place in the age of new self-consciousness, and
therefore calling up wickedness from the depths both in
his soul and in Lady Macbeth's; Lear, wilfulness and
blindness to the inner realities of those around him;
Coriolanus, the pride and passion characterised by
Professor Dowden as "the mob in his own nature";
Antony and Cleopatra, excess of luxury (in the Elizabethan sense); Timon, unbridled generosity.
Rudolf Steiner says of this period:
"When Shakespeare has created *Hamlet*, a kind of
bitterness towards the external physical world comes
over him. We feel as though he were living in other
worlds and judging the physical world differently,
looking down from the point of view of other worlds.
From this inner deepening of experience, with all its
inner tragedy, we see him emerge again. First he has
learned the external dramatic medium, then he has gone
through deepest inwardness, what I would call the
meeting with the World Spirit of which Goethe spoke so
beautifully. Now he enters life once again with a certain
humour, and his work carries in it the loftiest spirituality
and the highest dramatic power – as, for example, in

The Tempest, one of the most wonderful creations of all mankind, one of the richest products of the evolution of dramatic art."[34]

In the period which opens with *Pericles*, we are aware of a new approach to the unseen worlds. Ghosts, for example, had been, in *Richard II*, *Hamlet*, *Macbeth*, uneasy spirits, crying out for vengeance. But in *Cymbeline* the dead parents and brothers of Posthumus become his helpers, bringing about Jupiter's intervention to "take off his miseries." (V, iv).

In the earlier plays of Shakespeare's merely theoretical Rosicrucianism, one might well have heard in such intervention the creaking of the antique mechanism of the *Deus ex Machina*. But in these last romances, Jupiter's visit to Posthumus, Apollo's oracle, Diana's appearance to Pericles, all speak of a coming closer to the spiritual worlds, of an acknowledgement that they are near enough to enter and to recreate the earthly one. To translate Mount Olympus into terms of Asgard, they intimate that the segregation of spirit from matter pictured in the Twilight of the Gods is beginning to draw towards its close.

We have seen in Lear the final titanic breakdown of the earlier universal ego-consciousness of the group-soul, involving man and Nature herself in shattering cata-clysms. We have seen in Hamlet the first birthpangs of the as yet weak individual ego, in Horatio that ego already "given", in Cordelia that ego mellowed and made firm in its own entity and integrity by suffering. This transition from universal ego-consciousness to that of the individual ego went hand in hand with the withdrawal from men's sight of the spirit ensouling Nature.

In ancient times it was only in the Mysteries that men

[34] SHAKESPEARE AND THE NEW IDEALS

had a feeling of selfhood, and that – as we saw in Chapter I – only as a foreshadowing. At that time physical phenomena were seen as interpenetrated by their archetypes. As man began to awaken, his sight grew clearer for perception of the sensible world and cloudier for that of the supersensible permeating it. In later Greece it was possible for men to achieve a temporary experience of the individual self and of individual thinking, but only at the cost of obliterating their perception of the spirit within matter. In doing this they were cut off from the fountains of life-forces in Nature which fed and refreshed them, and felt worn-out and weary. It was in order to be made well again that they witnessed the Tragedies, in which pity and terror, compassion and awe, acted therapeutically.

"Men said to themselves: 'When one begins to feel one's ego, the world becomes empty of the gods. The Drama places the gods once more before us.' It was a representation of the spiritual that prevails behind the world."[35]

The earliest beginnings of Tragedy (in 534 B.C.) depicted the sufferings on behalf of Man of the god Dionysos, the Mystery-bringer of the first gleams of ego-consciousness. He was the only character; his soul-sufferings were described in odes to the Chorus, grouped about him as satyrs clad in goatskins (hence the name, Tragedy, from *tragodia*, goat-odes). In the chariot of the priest Thespis, Dionysos and the Chorus were driven along the Sacred Way from the Mystery-Temple at Eleusis to Athens, twelve miles away, where, at the foot of the Acropolis, this tragedy was originally presented from the chariot of Thespis, which was thus the first public stage of the Western world. (It is interesting in this connection to remember the pageant-stage of the medieval Mystery-Cycles.)

[35] Rudolf Steiner: CHANGES IN HUMAN WORLD-CONCEPTION

In 525 B.C., nine years after the first appearance of
Dionysos on this chariot-stage, Æschylos was born.
While he was still a boy he had a dream in which
Dionysos appeared to him, saying:
"Thee, Æschylos, have I chosen to bring my Mysteries
forth from their sanctuary. For man is now ripe to
experience more fully the workings of the ego."
So, with the action and the number of characters in-
creased, Greek Drama as we know it in the plays of
Æschylos was born. With Æschylos and with Sophocles,
this Drama still retained Tragedy's original function of
bringing about a healing crisis in the spectators and
presenting to them "the spiritual which prevails behind
the world". Only with the more intellectualised Euripides and a more intellectualised Greece did the Drama
begin to lose its therapeutic content and so gradually to
decline into a mere form of entertainment.

When Nature had become for man a corpse bereft of
soul and spirit, what had been experienced prophetically
in the Tragedy of Dionysos became, in the Crucifixion on
Golgotha, a real event in World-History. "Now men
conceived the impulse, through the dawning intellect, to
comprehend in One that which is scattered through all
Nature. And they did comprehend it so, in the dead
Christ-Jesus on the Cross. All spirituality man sees when
he directs his vision to the fact that there arose out of this
body the living Christ, in whose Being every human soul
can henceforth partake …

"Man once felt nature around him filled everywhere
with soul and spirit. In later times he felt the power to
perceive his own 'I am' over against the Nature that was
now bereft of soul. In compensation, he required the
picture of the God that is in man, and he felt this picture
in the Dionysos presented to him in the scenes of the

Greek Drama. Then, in a still later time, he still felt
Nature around him void of soul, and the 'I am' within
him. The Drama now became Fact. The Cross arose on
Golgotha; and at the same time what man had originally
lost arose again in his own inner being, as the 'Not I,
but Christ in me'." [36]

Bacon, Newton and the long line of scientists and techno-
logists descended from them have made Nature a corpse
many times over; on this the Lear ego-consciousness of
our age is firmly founded. But now, out of St. Paul's "Not
I, but Christ in me," it is part of man's future task   to
experience material substance once more as an expression of the spiritual, to fill once more everything of an
earthly character with a spiritual content, and by adding
to sense reality the spiritual reality behind it, to achieve
the full reality.

Against this background, we see that in depicting Lear
with the dead Cordelia in his arms, Shakespeare has
brought forth into the light of our own age a mighty
archetypal picture. Michaelangelo has in the same period
also placed it before us in his Pieta – in this Body taken
down from the Cross is gathered all the spirituality of
which our unchristened ego-consciousness and its intellectual thinking have deprived matter. But the Body *is*
taken down from the Cross and is on its way to its nest
of spice in Joseph's virgin sepulchre; it is in transition
from Phoenix-death to Phoenix-resurrection. And since
for the Earth as well as for mankind Good Friday is
followed by Easter morning, through the corpse of Nature
also can spirit again be made manifest; but in this
resurrection man must be a co-creator.

In Lear's arms – in the arms of the old universal con-
sciouness – Cordelia, the higher aspect of the young ego,
lies dead, slain by the death-forces in Edmund, that

---

[36] Rudolf Steiner, *Op. cit.*

ego's darker side. But then the picture changes into that of Arviragus with Imogen not dead but sleeping in his arms – Imogen, so like in character to the Cordelia of the end of *King Lear* that one thinks of her as Cordelia reborn. In Imogen, that "piece of tender air," it is the sleeping future that Arviragus bears.

Cordelia's blessing, with some aspect of her likeness, rests, in fact, on all the young generation of Shakespeare's final group of plays. Imogen, Marina, Perdita, Miranda – they are all lovely and innocent, having a sisterly likeness, yet each an individual. They belong to an entirely different world from that of that earlier group of sisters, Rosalind, Beatrice, Viola, Olivia. For they are Shakespeare's new humanity; and with all their individual differences they have one thing in common – they are all beings whose dreams of matter will come through the gates of horn.

That awareness of the salt-forming process which had begun in Lear as a negative picture of the destructiveness of the passions and a loathing of sex has in this last group of plays progressed into the positive picture of ardent chastity – so positive a picture that Marina, the first of this new generation, penetrates redemptively into the very citadel of lust itself.

Pericles characterises her in arresting words:

> *Falseness cannot come from thee, for thou look'st*
> *Modest as justice, and thou seem'st a palace*
> *For the crown'd truth to dwell in ... Thou dost look*
> *Like Patience gazing on king's graves, and smiling*
> *Extremity out of act.*
>
> *(Pericles, V, i)*

She unites the clear consciousness which should be a fruit

of our own era with so plant-pure a nature that she can remain untarnished in a brothel, and even awaken the higher selves of others there. Hers could be called a Manichean marriage. Taken on a romantic and external level, her union with the by no means spotless Lysimachus would not please us; but she is the first-born of this new generation; she must unite with what is older to form a bridge. By the time Perdita and Miranda are born, in Florizel and Ferdinand bridegrooms have been reared to match them.

In view of this new generation's destiny, it is significant that Marina brings a new stream of culture to Mitylene, and that for Pericles she unlocks again the creative forces of the Word. The great glory of the marriage between Thaisa and Pericles is that it has given birth to a fairer creature than themselves.

Imogen's path, like Marina's, leads through trials and sufferings. Posthumus' jealousy, the Queen's evil designs, and Cloten's lust drive her forth from her father's palace, disguised as a page, to experience that homelessness which is a stage on the Mystery-path of development. Through all her tribulations there shines forth from her an inner soul-quality of such loveliness that one recognizes in her, as in Marina, one of those spirits, sensed by Keats,

"standing apart
Upon the forehead of the age to come.
These, these will give the world another heart."

So will her two brothers, the princely twins Arviragus and Guiderius, who have been brought up in the caves of the Welsh mountains, sequestered from a corrupt society, and whose training in reverence, courage, uprightness, brotherliness, has prepared them for a life of ethical activity when they return to court.

Perdita, like them, has been reared simply, in country surroundings, far from the sophistication of courts, so that her Persephone-forces have been guarded and remain so radiant and robust that her mere presence brings about a miracle of resurrection in Hermione, setting her frozen life-currents aflow again. Perdita's royal blood marries so kindly with her rural breeding that "all her acts are queens" (IV, v), and she herself

> *The most peerless piece of earth, I think,*
> *That e'er the sun shone bright on.*
>
> *(V, i)*

And, last-born, most admir'd Miranda. she to whose presence Paradise adheres, dewdrop-clear, divinely artless, full of wonder and compassion. And as in her that compassion, which Cordelia reached only through suffering, is already a "given" quality, so also already "given" is that organ of a new clear insight which Lear had had to fashion out of agony. In the black coal of Sebastian and Antonio she sees spontaneously the immortal diamond. Already she, like Marina, is a seed-bearer of a future Manicheism.

Man has long been estranged from his own divine archetype; but in Shakespeare's group of youngest sons and daughters one feels that man and archetype are beginning to grow each towards the other. In descending to earth, his rose's shadow went through a Fall; but this new humanity points to a future when rose's shadow shall be so transparent for true rose that the two shall be as one.

Where has one met such young human beings before?
One has heard rumours of them, very faint and far away,
in a prophecy which came forth from the Northern
Mysteries:

> *"Lif and Lifthrasir*   *lie hidden*
> *In Hoddmimir's Wood.*
> *Morning dew*   *all their meat.*
> *From them stems a new race."* [37]

During the Twilight of the Gods, when men no longer
see the working of the spiritual in the material, Lif and
Lifthrasir – Life and Bearer-of-Life – are preserved in the
Wood of Mimir. Mimir is the ruler of runes that reveal
the spirit of Nature, the guardian of Odin's eye, that
supersensory sight which withdraws from men in the
Twilight. *Hodd*, cognate with *Hoard*, means *treasure*;
Mimir's treasure, laid up in this wood, is Odin's eye, this
sleeping supersensory sight.
The Twilight will end when the silent god, Vidar,
speaks; man's renewed vision of the spiritual permeating
the physical is thus bound up with a new annunciation
of the Creative Word. We find this connection also clearly
intimated in Greek pre-Christian thought, where, while
in Heraclitus the Logos is the First Cause and Prime
Mover of the universe, Plato uses the plural, Logoi, of
the archetypes producing all that is perceptible,
When Vidar speaks, Nature will be recreated:

> *"Now do I see*   *the earth anew*
> *Rise all green*   *from the waves again."* [38]

[37] VAFTHRUDISMAL, in the Poetic Edda
[38] VOLUSPA, in the Poetic Edda

The spirituality which had been visibly at work in
Nature in earlier times will come forth into the light
again on a new level. And at the same time, *Voluspa*
tells us:

> *"Then from above   shall there come forth*
> *The Mighty One   who governs all things."*

It is clear that by this is not meant the first coming of
Christianity to the North; for the Northern Initiates'
prophetic sight made them aware that this Roman
Christianity would play a part in the downfall of their
gods, would help to precipitate the Twilight during
which the Northern Nature-Mysteries would be transformed into sense-revelation. But beyond the Twilight
there would come a time when not only the Logoi would
become perceptible, but with them the Logos Himself.
"The Mighty One comes forth from above," *Voluspa* tells
us; and The Apocalypse, "Behold, he cometh with clouds;
and every eye shall see him."
When man's vision embraces both worlds, then natural
science and the divine will be united; then perception of
the spiritual becomes a new natural-scientific faculty.
And of these Lifs and Lifthrasirs, these Marinas and
Imogens and Perditas and Mirandas, George Meredith
tells us that

> *"They shall lift up their Earth to meet her Lord,*
> *Themselves the attuning chord." [39]*

"In Dante the human ego was grasped in the profoundest

[39] HYMN TO COLOUR

depths of the soul. In Shakespeare the ego issues from the interior soul and enters other souls. In Goethe we see the ego issuing from itself and finding its way into the spiritual world."[40]

Goethe is aware from direct experiences of the coming end of the Twilight. Shakespeare comforts us with its promise. His youngest sons and daughters await it in the Hoddmimir's Wood. And he himself, in *The Tempest*, dreams his own dream of it. For here, like Hermia in the Wood near Athens, he sees with parted eye, when everything seems double. Nothing could be more concrete than his details of Nature on the island –

> *I prithee, let me bring thee where crabs grow;*
> *And I with my long nails will dig thee pignuts;*
> *Show thee a jay's nest and instruct thee how*
> *To snare the nimble marmozet; I'll bring thee*
> *To clustering filberts and sometimes I'll get thee*
> *Young scamels from the rock. Wilt thou go with me?*
>
> (II, ii)

And yet Prospero knows that cloud-capp'd palaces are roses' shadows. In *The Tempest* Shakespeare brings soul's history and life's labour to a majestic climax, painting the secrets of matter in words as Constable did in colours:

> *"His sunburst inspiration*
> *Made earthly forms so true*
> *To life, so new to vision,*
> *That now the actual view*
> *Seems a mere phantom, through*
> *Whose blur we glimpse creation"* [41]

[40] Rudolf Steiner, METAMORPHOSES OF THE SOUL
[41] Cecil Day Lewis, DEDHAM VALE

Such then was Shakespeare's flowering of the spirit. What of the fruit of this flowering?

Shakespeare never himself published a play, and only two of his poems – *Venus and Adonis* and *The Rape of Lucrece*. For it was then customary for plays to be sold outright to a theatre for £5 to £10 each; and the theatre never printed them, since that would make the text generally available. When Ben Johnson brought out his own *Collected Works* in 1616 (the year of Shakespeare's death), it was the first time such a thing had ever happened in England and his action provoked violent condemnation throughout literary society, where it was regarded as dishonourable for a playwright to sell his work twice over, first to a theatre and then to a bookseller. Even as late as 1630, Thomas Heywood virtuously puts it on record that *he* has not been guilty of this misdemeanour.

But shorthand, another symptom of the new intellectualising of the age, had recently made its appearance, and shorthand writers often pirated garbled and mutilated versions of new plays by taking down passages under cover of their cloaks during a performance. This was the origin of the "Corrupt Quartos", mangled editions of some of Shakespeare's plays which were printed during his lifetime without his knowledge or permission.

In 1623, seven years after Shakespeare's death, the First Folio of his plays, based on the original Globe playscripts, was brought out, dedicated to the Earl of Pembroke, now Lord Chamberlain, and his brother, the Earl of Montgomery. In that same year a large international gathering of Rosicrucians had been held in Paris, attended by many leading English members of the order; and it has been suggested that it was from this source that the impulse for this publication came.[42] Certainly

[42] W. F. C. Wigston, *Op. cit.*

none could have been more aware than the Rosicrucians
of that time that it was Christian Rosenkreutz who stood
behind Shakespeare at his desk, as in old Greek ikons
angels stand behind the Evangelists at theirs; and none
could have been more aware than they that into his
plays had been poured nurture to meet more than contemporary needs and that it was a demand of destiny
that they should be made available to posterity in as
nearly as possible an authentic form.

John Heminge and Henry Condell, the First Folio's
editors, had been Shakespeare's fellow-actors and co-
housekeepers (Heminge had been the first Falstaff); they
had also long been the business managers of The Globe.
Shakespeare's Will breathes a warm regard for them,
together with Richard Burbage, that minister of Fate
who had directed his steps to London:

"Twentysix shillings and eightpence each wherewith to
buy a ring in memory of the deceased to my comrades,
John Heminge, Richard Burbage and Henry Condell."

They write in their Preface:

"Where before you were abused with divers stolen and
surreptitious copies, maimed and deformed by the frauds
and stealths of injurious imposters, even those are now
offered to your view cured and perfect and absolute in
their numbers as he conceived them, who, as he was a
happy imitator of Nature, was a most gentle expresser of
it. His mind and hand went together; and what he
thought he uttered with that earnestness that we have
scarce received from him a blot in his papers" – which
conjures up a pleasant picture of Shakespeare's com-
radely co-housekeepers joyfully receiving a new playscript from his hands.

Though it presents certain anomalies (for example, while
omitting *Pericles*, entered in the Stationers' Register as by

Shakespeare in 1608, it includes *Henry VIII*, in which other hands are also evident), the First Folio is the immediate instrument of Shakespeare's later fruiting; not only are its versions of the Quarto-plays less corrupt than these, but it also includes nineteen of his plays which would otherwise have been unknown to us.

At the Restoration, when returning Royalty brought French classicism to England, Shakespeare suffered an eclipse. The Age of Reason, also, engaged in the development of quite other faculties than imagination, could only applaud him when it had tailored and tortured him into its own likeness. But the Age of the Novel, with its accent on characterization, rediscovered him as the master of the drama concerned with the individual; since when each successive change in consciousness has valued him so highly and so increasingly for how he speaks to its own condition, that "from the nineteenth century on, the five individuals who have most influenced the spiritual education of the West are: David, Homer, Dante, Goethe, Shakespeare – what found expression *through* Shakespeare, even if not *in* Shakespeare himself."[43]

Today, methods of cognition are again undergoing a quiet and gradual transformation. The Intellect waits for us to warm it into Imagination. The spectator consciousness is reaching out to become once more a participating consciousness, not, as before, within the group-soul, but in the individual. The increase of extra-sensory perception on many levels brings us intimations of a new faculty whose organ is in process of being fashioned.

So we today are equipped to penetrate, if we will, with washed eyes and Mermaid alertness, to depths of inwardness in Shakespeare's plays of which the intervening centuries were not so fully aware. Like the hierophant in the Mysteries, like the true alchemist in his laboratory,

---

[43] Rudolf Steiner, THE GOSPEL OF ST. MARK

Shakespeare is able, in his characters, to live through great dramas of the soul; and we today have been newly gifted with the capacity to live through these dramas with him.

If we confine ourselves to a purely exoteric reading of his plays, we touch only the outermost fringe of what he has to give us; if we place his deep understanding of life in the light of the Mystery-wisdom which was its distant source, we come to a greater clarity as to how and where we ourselves stand in the great sweep of evolution and as to what the future of mankind demands of us.

"Showing thus the derivation of Drama from the Ancient Mysteries, and its purpose as a living education of mankind, we understand how it is that such an educative power goes out from Shakespeare's plays ...

"There lies in Shakespeare's dramatic art a power which ever and again not only gives us fresh enthusiasm but kindles in us, from our imagination and in our spiritual nature, our own creative powers ...

"The receiving of Shakespeare into our mind and soul can give us as men and women of today the power, the inner impulse, to follow spiritual ideals ...

"Shakespeare gave all humanity a great inspiration towards the new ideals of mankind."[44]

So what, in *The Tempest*, two of the three men of sin said in insolent jest concerning holy Gonzalo, we may say in marvelling earnestness of Shakespeare:

ANTONIO: *His word is more than the miraculous harp.*
SEBASTIAN: *He hath rais'd the wall, and houses, too.*
ANTONIO: *What impossible matter will he make*
easy next?

[44] Rudolf Steiner, SHAKESPEARE AND THE NEW IDEALS

SEBASTIAN: *I think he will carry this island home in his pocket, and give it his son for an apple.*
ANTONIO: *And, sowing the kernels of it in the sea, bring forth more islands.*
ALONSO: *Ay?*

(II, i)

It rests with our creative response to erase Alonso's question-mark.

OUTLINE OF THE CHYMICAL WEDDING

ON Easter Eve, 1459, Christian Rosenkreutz was sitting in his cottage on a hillside in meditation, when an angelic messenger brought him an invitation to the Royal Wedding. The letter, however, contained a warning that one who weighed too light, or was not pure of soul, would do well not to accept.

During the night he had a dream which he interpreted as being an encouragement to undertake the journey; so next day he set out for the castle.

He reached and passed through the two outer portals successfully and was met, just as dusk was falling, by a Virgin in blue bearing a light, who guided him into the castle.

In due course he found himself in a great hall where a large concourse of guests were gathered – emperors, kings, lords were there, but also men he knew whom he had held in little esteem and was surprised they should have been invited.

When the bell rang to summon them to the feast, there was a scramble for the highest places and Christian Rosenkreutz found himself at the lowermost table.

The noisy guests at the top began boasting of their occult powers; one heard the music of the spheres, another could see Plato's ideas, and so on.

After the feast, delicate music was heard and the Virgin reappeared clad in dazzling white and gold.

She welcomed the guests in the name of the young King, and warned them that next morning they would be weighed to see whether they were worthy to attend the wedding.

On the morning of the third day the Virgin again entered the great hall, this time clad in red velvet and wearing a laurel wreath. She was followed by men bearing great golden scales and seven weights, some of which were unbelievably heavy.

The emperors were first weighed, and all except one were found to be too light to pass the test. The successful one was clothed in red velvet, given a laurel wreath, and invited by the Virgin to sit on the steps of her throne. Very few of the crowd were successful in passing the test and Christian Rosenkreutz waited in trepidation for his turn. When it came at last, it was found that he outstayed all the weights and in addition the weight of three knight in full armour – whereupon one of the pages cried out in a loud voice "That is he".

At the meal which followed, the few guests who had been accepted, now clad in crimson robes with laurel wreaths, were seated at the high table. The young King sent to each as a gift the Insignia of the Order of the Golden Fleece.

Afterwards, most of the guests who had failed were dismissed, receiving a draught of forgetfulness at the gate. The cheats and imposters, however, lost their lives.

At supper time there was much lively talk and riddles were propounded. The Virgin gave them a riddle which contained her name and invited them to guess it. Christian Rosenkreutz guessed correctly; it was Alchimia. On the fourth day, they were led by the Virgin and her musicians up 365 steps to the chamber where sat the young King and Queen. The guests were welcomed in the King's name by old Atlas. The royal couple wore laurel wreaths and over their heads hung two golden crowns. On their right sat an old King with his young Queen; on the left a black King, middle-aged, with a "dainty old matron" at his side.

The young King then invited his guests to see "a merry comedy". It opened with an old King finding a little chest floating on the sea, which contained a baby princess, heiress to a neighbouring kingdom, who had been stolen by the Moors.

He had her carefully brought up, and planned to marry her to his son when she was of age. More than once she fell again into the hands of the Moorish king, who cast her into prison and ill-treated her. She was finally rescued by the young prince and restored to her kingdom.

The marriage was held amid great rejoicings and the play closed with a wedding hymn calling down blessing on the young couple and praying that a fairer future race might spring from them.

When the guests returned to the King's chamber the three royal couples looked very solemn and were dressed in black. The guests swore an oath of fealty to the young King.

At the tolling of a bell, six coffins were brought in and

placed in the centre of the room. The Virgin bound the eyes of the Kings and Queens with black scarves, and finally the Moor strode into the room, carrying an axe.

One after another the royal couples were beheaded by the Moor. Each head was reverently wrapped in a black cloth and the blood caught in a golden cup. Finally, the Moor was himself beheaded and his head placed in a little shrine.

As they watched these sad happenings the guests wept, but Alchimia bade them be of good cheer.

"The lives of these Kings and Queens", she said, "stand now in your hands. If you will but follow me, this death shall make many to live."

The next morning the Virgin invited the guest to accompany her across the lake to the Tower of Olympus, to assist in preparing the medicaments which would restore the royal couple to life. The coffins had already been conveyed there during the night – the guests now followed in small ships. On the way, they had to pass the sirens, who sang to them seductively and sweetly, awakening thoughts of earthly love and passion.

Arrived at the Tower, the guests were taken to an underground laboratory, to prepare herbs and crush precious stones.

There were seven storeys to the Tower, on each of which the guests assisted in complicated alchemical processes connected with the bodies of the Kings and Queens and the head of the Moor. Each stage is accompanied by music.

Christian Rosenkreutz and three other specially favoured guests are allowed to ascend to a turret on the eighth floor, where they are witnesses of the last stage of the rebirth. They see, lying side by side, two perfect images of the young King and Queen, very small, angelically fair and transparent. The images are fed with the blood of a bird and grow until they reach their perfect full growth. They are now of unspeakable beauty. Then, with ceremonial gestures and with music the royal couple are restored to life.

They are escorted downstairs to the boats and set sail for home.

The next day the wedding guests rejoin them. They find the young King and Queen playing a game not unlike chess, where good forces are pitted against evil.

The young King makes the wedding guests Knights of the Golden Stone – they have to take five vows, one of which was to use their talents freely in the service of all who have need of them.

Christian Rosenkreutz is appointed Keeper of the Gate and is given a gold ring and bidden to be faithful to his trust.

*   *   *   *   *   *

The above is a brief abstract of a part of this complex and fascinating story, insofar as it concerns the work of Shakespeare. Readers interested in the full story and its meaning are referred to *A Commentary on the Chymical Wedding of Christian Rosenkreutz*, by Margaret Bennell and Isabel Wyatt, obtainable from Hawkwood College, Stroud, Glos.